The Cadbury Code and Recurrent Crisis

"A fascinating book, tracing the development of the UK Corporate Governance Code and highlighting its continuity through successive crises. It identifies areas of controversy and challenge, intriguingly suggesting that 'defeated logics' are merely suspended, perhaps poised to return. Essential interdisciplinary reading for all those interested in the UK's corporate governance system."

—Andrew Johnston, *Professor of Company Law and Corporate Governance, School of Law, University of Warwick*

"The importance of the Cadbury Committee and the codes of corporate governance that followed in shaping the current form and scope of possibility for corporate governance in the UK can hardly be underestimated. Nordberg's fascinating account of the process by which these have been shaped by individuals and institutions is a welcome examination of how the code developed over time, what it achieved, and what it left undone. Those who care about how boards of directors work and how that work is guided by policy can learn much from this study."

—Dr. Jeroen Veldman, *Associate Professor, Nyenrode Business University, The Netherlands*

"Professor Nordberg provides a timely and thoughtful discussion on a topic which, if anything, is even more important than it was some three decades ago. Recurrent corporate governance crises indeed indicate that the current paradigmatic approach to good corporate governance, with its focus on internal control, risk management, audit, overseen by a board, and increasingly dependent on the contribution of the independent director, may provide limited assurance as to its ability to prevent further cases of governance failures. Since the early 1990s we have seen increasingly damaging examples of governance failures which must give rise to the question whether the various corporate governance codes, guides, laws and formal reviews address the core problem of governance, how to prevent those entrusted with the assets of others from abusing their position, to a satisfactory degree. This is not purely an academic concern. Gross failures of governance can touch upon the livelihoods of entire nations and increasingly impact on the global community through the concept of ecological governance which aims at incorporating issues of biodiversity and species extinction into the heart of the governance model. The late Sir Adrian Cadbury created an admirable and world leading guide to best governance practice, setting in motion a process of continuously reviewing, refining, and updating a Code which endured the test of time and is adopted across many jurisdictions. Nordberg's book strongly contributes to the debate on how to address an age-old problem in a rapidly changing environment. By reflecting on current insights, urging to learn from past mistakes, emphasising a broad discussion, and most of all, keeping an open mind to potential future solutions, Nordberg continues the great tradition of asking critical questions without necessarily providing predetermined answers."

—Oliver Marnet *is Associate Professor in Accounting at the Southampton Business School, who has written extensively on corporate governance and external audit, and has provided written evidence to BEIS, CMA, ICSA, ICAEW, PIRC, the European Commission, and the FRC's Guidance on Board Effectiveness*

Donald Nordberg

The Cadbury Code and Recurrent Crisis

A Model for Corporate Governance?

palgrave
macmillan

Donald Nordberg
Bournemouth University Business School
Bournemouth, UK

ISBN 978-3-030-55221-3 ISBN 978-3-030-55222-0 (eBook)
https://doi.org/10.1007/978-3-030-55222-0

This Palgrave Macmillan imprint is published by the registered company Springer Nature Switzerland AG
The registered company address is: Gewerbestrasse 11, 6330 Cham, Switzerland

Acknowledgements

The ideas in this book grew from the observations of many scholars and practitioners I have known or whose work I have found stimulating. At the time of the Cadbury deliberations, I was an editorial executive for the news agency Reuters, then based in New York. There we were preoccupied by the collapse of the Soviet Union and an emerging economic order based on triumphant capitalism. As journalists, however, we could not escape the concern for colleagues when Robert Maxwell's two UK-listed corporations—Mirror Group Newspapers and Maxwell Communication—collapsed. Also, Maxwell had sat as non-executive director on the Reuters board as it listed on the London Stock Exchange and rapidly moved into the FTSE100 index, serving alongside his arch-rival Rupert Murdoch.

But there was more. The demise of Maxwell's companies was foreshadowed by fraudulent use of their pension funds to prop up his faltering share prices. Those who lost their retirement savings included reporters and editors at the New York *Daily News*, which Maxwell owned. For journalists, this governance failure was personal. When I returned to London a few years later, I discovered that a strange term—'corporate governance'—had entered the everyday discourse, not just of investors and corporate directors, but of journalists as well.

By the time 'Cadbury' morphed into the 'Combined Code', I was involved in shareholder relations and met Bernard Taylor at Henley Management College, who convened an annual conference on board effectiveness. There I got to know the famous US activist investor and author Robert A.G. Monks. Through Tomorrow's Company—a project of the Royal Society of the Arts—I joined debates about reforming company law. I also met the governance academics at the Business School at City University of London, among them Georges Selim and Rob Melville. They introduced me to Terry McNulty from the University of Liverpool, who had led a research project for the 2003 Higgs Review. He supervised my doctoral studies, which commenced just as the global financial crisis began. This book revisits themes from that study and includes sections adapted from an article in *Economics and Business Review* for a special issue on corporate governance co-edited by my colleague at Bournemouth University, Steve Letza, and used here with permission.

Other helpful suggestions came from Kevin Tennant, Suzanne Konzelmann, Jeroen Veldman, David Gindis, Dionysia Katelouzou, Gerhard Schnyder, and Lez Rayman-Bacchus. They all listened to aspects of the research that led to this volume and provided insights and encouragement. Any mistakes, however, are my own.

September 2020 Donald Nordberg

Prologue

Since 1992, corporate governance in the UK and much of the world has been articulated in codes of conduct, rather than formal law and regulations or even less formal social arrangements. Moreover, despite their gradual revision over the years, their core tenets survived despite repeated and arguably growing shocks to the system they were meant to protect. That suggests the problems they sought to address have not been solved. Britain—in particular its banks—was perhaps the worst hit by the global financial crisis, at a cost to the state that continues more than a decade later. How did various revisions fail to undertake fresh approaches to the recurring crises?

This book explores how corporate governance in Britain came to be codified, what key disputes took place during its major revisions, and how it institutionalised a way of viewing what corporate governance should be. This study also suggests that the while the flexibility that was built into the code's compliance regime allowed for variations, few companies took the opportunities provided to experiment with other ways of organisation the work of boards of directors. The code is much admired, with good reason. And it has achieved wide legitimacy. But is it the model for corporate governance?

The Cadbury Code and Report was the starting point for this new direction. It combined a set of principles of good governance that served as a how to guide for listed companies. It established a regulatory framework that guided equity capital markets and proposed ways that shareholders—principally institutional investors—should relate to the companies in which they invest. This framework was loose because of a central plank of the code: it was to be voluntary, subject the requirement that companies explain why they decided not to comply. Although the Cadbury Code did not use the phrase, this idea quickly attracted the label 'comply-or-explain'.

Moreover, the influence of this domestic exercise was vast. The code's ideas were copied in countries around the world, from France to South Africa to Germany, then to much of Africa and South America, and to Russia and Japan. One of its core tenets even found its way into the listing requirements of the New York Stock Exchange and Nasdaq, despite wide criticism from American CEOs: the provision concerning the separation of roles of the company chair and the chief executive officer (CEO), to prevent one person having 'unfettered' boardroom control. There, too, 'comply-or-explain' applied.

The code's influence grew even larger. Its principles informed other codes, often written by professional bodies for a wide range of organisation types far removed from the world of capital markets, investment portfolios, and even shareholders.

The UK code of corporate governance is widely admired and imitated, but it has not prevented the types of emergency that led to its creation—recurring failures of large corporations because of the lack of oversight and internal control. The biggest case was the financial crisis of 2007–2009, in which the UK suffered disproportionate damage, as we shall see.

Were we expecting too much of a code of conduct? Why did the framers of the code not recommend something stronger than a voluntary code of conduct?

This study examines those questions through analysis of the debates that led up to the drafting of the original Cadbury Code and then the major revisions undertaken in 2003 and 2010 in response to renewed crises. It does so through a critical discourse analysis of contributions to the consultations that informed the drafting, undertaken against the economic and political context that shaped the code and was then shaped by it.

It shows, historically, how the process engaged actors from all parts of the chain of investment, and how that process embedded power in the hands of central actors. Theoretically, it shows how the logics employed in the debate became institutionalised, but also how the form of their institutionalisation provided opportunities for change, leaving rejected logics suspended not defeated, so they could resurface later, which enhanced the legitimacy of the process. Practically, it demonstrates how the code's flexibility forestalled more radical action and won acceptance even among those whose views it rejected.

The crisis in corporate governance is one MacAvoy and Millstein call 'recurrent'. 'The turnaround began taking place in the mid-1990s ... The die was cast for effective governance through board structure and process and we could move on ... but the new form was not universally and instantaneously followed by changes in conduct' (2003, pp. 2–3). They were writing just as US financial markets had just been rocked by failures of very large corporations, the collapse of the market in new technology companies, and the implosion of one of the five global accountancy and audit firms. They expressed their concern that the responses, in regulation and corporate behaviour would prove disappointing. There was some change in US practice, which included translating some aspects of UK corporate governance into US listing requirements. Yet before the decade was out, both countries would experience an even more serious corporate governance crisis.

This study examines how the UK reforms, enacted in the 1990s and repeatedly revised, kept options for different responses open to debate but nonetheless left them unexplored in practice. It questions what might have happened if the roads not taken had been followed, perhaps as experiments rather than policy, and if in practice the code had been followed with the degrees of freedom that its language of explanation proposed. Instead of striving for formal compliance, and thus escape enforcement via investors and the proxy voting agencies they employed, corporate boards might have adopted a more thoughtful approach. They might have adapted code recommendations and innovated in board design and process to suit the peculiar circumstances of the company, rather than shaping the board and its processes to fit the code. What sort of ethos might then have developed?

Reference

MacAvoy, P., & Millstein, I. (2003). *The recurrent crisis: in corporate governance*. Basingstoke: Palgrave Macmillan.

Contents

About the Author

Donald Nordberg is Associate Professor at Bournemouth University in the UK and author of *Corporate Governance: Principles and Issues* (Sage, 2011). His research has been published in many journals, including *Corporate Governance: An International Review, Business History, Leadership, Journal of Financial Regulation and Compliance, European Management Journal,* and *Philosophy of Management*. He is also a governance practitioner: chair of a major UK social care provider and non-executive director of a company in the performing arts. Earlier he was a correspondent and editorial executive at Reuters, based in London, Frankfurt, Zurich, and New York. A native of Chicago, he was educated in the US at Reed College in Portland, Oregon, and the University of Illinois at Urbana-Champaign, and in Britain at the Universities of Warwick and Liverpool.

List of Figures

List of Tables

CHAPTER 1

Successes in Corporate Governance—Or Failures?

Abstract Codes of corporate governance around the world have drawn inspiration from the UK's Cadbury Code and its subsequent iterations. This widely admired and imitated regulative measure emerged from a crisis in corporate governance and was designed in part to prevent corporation collapses. In the past three decades, however, corporate collapses have continued and even intensified in impact. The chapter asks: In what ways has codifying corporate governance succeeded? In what ways has it failed?

Keywords Codes of corporate governance · Success · Failure

For nearly 30 years, corporate governance in the UK—and in the many countries that followed its lead—has been defined in terms of a code of conduct. It was a project conceived in a crisis and then gestated through long processes of consultation, drafting, more consultation, further drafting. It was an effort that engaged the sceptical, confronted the hostile, and eventually won over a large body of believers, many who have invested time, talent, and faith in both the code and the process through which it was created.

The decision to codify what constitutes good, or even best, practice in corporate governance is frequently seen as a masterstroke of regulatory genius. Though its authors could not have anticipated it at the

D. Nordberg, *The Cadbury Code and Recurrent Crisis*,
https://doi.org/10.1007/978-3-030-55222-0_1

outset, this voluntary arrangement—with very little punishment possible for non-compliance—has all but extinguished pressure for what might have been the alternative: a regime of regulation with tough civil or criminal sanctions. But that does not mean that all is well.

Veldman and Willmott (2016), for example, warn of the limits of soft regulation, like codes. What they call the 'reflexive governance' of codes and comply or explain 'promises to forestall potential pathologies and crises that threaten confidence in corporate governance, and so bestows upon the Code a degree of credibility and legitimacy'. At the same time, however, it 'supports a particular, financialized political economy where the claims of wider constituencies are marginalized or even excluded' (Veldman & Willmott, 2016, p. 583). Their observations highlight a central problem in corporate governance and codes, however. As we shall explore, if the freedom of explanation as a means of compliance leads to reflexive, double-loop learning then it holds the promise of innovative and even transformative governance. If it degenerates into surface compliance and embeds power relationships, it can squeeze out other voices, lose insights that mayvan benefit the company, and in time sap the legitimacy of the code and the corporation. The alternative—hard regulation, with legal enforcement to ensure those 'wider constituencies' share power—risks creating a regime that lacks flexibility to respond to changing contexts.

This was a code fashioned for a particular crisis, in a particular country, at a particular stage in the evolution of its capital markets, and at particularly febrile moment in the politics of Britain. Yet that code—initially named The Cadbury Code, after its principal author, the late Sir Adrian Cadbury—has been widely imitated across geographies, institutional systems, and market contexts. The principles it established have found their way into codes written for other organisational types as well. Charities, trade associations, neighbourhood committees, government departments, and even parliament itself have copied its key recommendations, sometimes verbatim. Those recommendations thus inform what are often labelled as 'corporate governance reports' by entities that have nothing else in common with the world of corporations, listed on stock exchanges, with diverse and dispersed shareholders, the world for which the code was designed.

Moreover, the process of its development has come to have many imitators. It came about through a temporary body, established outside government, without statutory grounding, with no power to compel participation in its fact-gathering. That unofficial, non-governmental rule-making body nonetheless gained legitimacy, and not just among those directly affected, but in the broader public as well. The Cadbury Committee held consultations, informal and formal, filtering ideas through a draft and then modifying the draft, and then building a timetable for reviewing the 'final' version two years later, and then roughly two years after that. The cycle of opportunities for revisions arose through custom and practice, not a stipulation of an expiry date, and it has persisted through nearly 30 years of practice. This winnowing and filtering and revisiting makes it a living document, constantly open to revision, a standard in perpetual motion that nonetheless provides an anchor to the way corporate governance works.

The language of the code and the discourse it created have evolved over time in ways that suggest that its various authors are not complacent (Nordberg & McNulty, 2013), but its core principles are remarkably unchanged. According to Price, Harvey, Maclean, and Campbell (2018, p. 1557) that stability shows the code 'is institutionally embedded and subject to institutional stasis'.

The original code (Cadbury, 1992) developed in response to a series of corporate failures, and its major revisions in 2003 and 2010 were motivated by similar and arguably more systemic problems in corporate governance. Indeed, the global financial crisis of 2007–2009 nearly paralysed the world's financial system and triggered a recession of a scale not seen since the 1930s. The UK was especially hard-hit, seeing its first run on a bank since the mid-nineteenth Century.[1] That bank was nationalised; and as the crisis spread around the world, Britain was forced to part-nationalise two much larger banks, one of which had claimed the distinction of being the world's largest.

The UK code has focused attention on improving board effectiveness, and it clearly succeeded in getting boards to work harder. The time commitment that directors make has expanded. Board committees meet more frequently, and board papers are generally more detailed. Remuneration of non-executive directors has grown too. Direct data on this is hard to come by across the time since the Cadbury Code, as reporting requirements came into place only towards the end of the

[1] A small bank: Northern Rock. Unlike other major economies, Britain escaped from both the Wall Street Crash of 1929 and the Great Financial Crisis of 1914 without a bank run. See Roberts (2014).

1990s. However, one study showed that during a period of modest inflation in the economy, from just before Enron imploded in 2001 to just after the worst of the post-financial crisis recession had passed, director fees for listed UK companies roughly doubled (Goh & Gupta, 2016). It also demonstrated, against the grain of 'tougher' governance, that fees increased more for well-connected non-executive directors, those with wide personal networks among directors of other companies, and rather less for those with characteristics that might lead them to hold management to account.

But if the ambition of codes of corporate governance is to forestall corporate collapse, how did the code—through repeated consultations and reformulation, over two decades—fail to seek out other solutions, even as experiments? Why haven't we seen more vigorous interventions—in law and regulation—with greater compulsion, to compensate for the deficiency of what is, in effect, a voluntary code? These questions resonate in fields of public and organisational policy well beyond corporate governance.

This study examines the first question through analysis of the discourse developed as the code was being created and how its major revisions were conducted. That analysis considers the economic and political context in which the code developed, as well as the language in which the debate was conducted and the resulting discourse it created. It addresses the second through context-driven interpretation of those findings, which then leads to unanswered questions that provide a direction for future research in corporate governance and other fields. It does so by considering the process through which the code became institutionalised and then came to be taken for granted as 'good' (Hodge, 2017), or even 'best' (Seidl, Sanderson, & Roberts, 2013) practice.

Many of the code's provisions won over hearts and minds quickly, conforming to common sense and confirming existing custom and practice at many listed companies. Boards are responsible for the business. They should challenge management. That means they need in general to be independent of management, though the definition of independence might be difficult to discern from the outside. Directors should be conscientious, paying close attention to the information they receive. To do justice to the big issues, the code specified that certain tasks should be delegated in the first instance to committees—remuneration, audit, and nominating new directors, including importantly the chief executive.

Somewhat controversial in 1992 was the stipulation that the role of chairman and chief executive should not be combined. At many companies, however, this practice was already in place, reducing opposition to the idea and making opponents seem self-serving, rather than serving shareholder interests. Even though empirical evidence of its benefit is mixed (Elsayed, 2007; Krause, Semadeni, & Cannella, 2014), this provision became a hallmark of good corporate governance around the world.

Over the years additional layers were added. A 1995 review of executive pay urged boards to pay greater attention to ensuring that executive directors were not involved in decisions over executive pay. A 1998 review discussed interactions with major shareholders, seeking ongoing and constructive dialogue. There were dangers in this, as such investors might become privy the inside information and then not be able to trade shares in the company, so investors were reluctant to get too involved.

Moreover, engagement with corporations was seen as expensive. Large institutional fund managers, with hundreds of companies in the portfolio and perhaps a thousand on the watch list, would require an army of analysts to keep track of the companies and then engage in dialogue. Companies would then face that army and their cacophony of opinions about what the company should do next. But the guidance was broad, non-specific, and easily avoided: 'comply-or-explain' is a very useful tool. These guidelines were added to the Cadbury provisions, creating in 1998 a 'Combined Code' on corporate governance (see Committee on Corporate Governance, 2000).

This was a relatively stress-free time in capital markets. The Labour government elected in 1997 had avoided much of the feared anti-business prescriptions, and after quickly setting in motion a major review of Company Law, it then delayed any changes for several years. It had come to appreciate the complexity and the depth of opposition. By 2003, however, after a global crisis in corporate governance, the institutional and market context would shift.

The 2001 collapse of Enron in the US, followed by WorldCom, Tyco, and others, revealed flaws in the US system. The outcome was a sharp legal and regulatory turn in the Sarbanes-Oxley Act (Library of Congress, 2002), which prescribed much greater disclosure and director duties, yet failed to address some of the key faults in governance exposed by Enron and others (Nordberg, 2008). Moreover, this proved not to be a US-specific crisis. Problems also arose in continental Europe

(Ahold, Parmalat), Australia (HIH Holdings), and elsewhere (Deakin & Konzelmann, 2004). While the UK was not directly affected in a big way, it was difficult for the government to let things stay the same. Company Law reform was back on the agenda, eventually taking effect from 2006, and placing specific duties on company directors for the first time (UK Government, 2007; UK Parliament, 2006). The corporate governance code would also undergo a major revision (FRC, 2003).

Minor revisions followed in 2006 and 2008, the latter published just as the global financial crisis struck, in which UK banks were among those most damaged, and for reasons that were as much home-grown as imported (Bank of England, 2015; FSA, 2011). A revision of the Combined Code, scheduled for 2010, was brought forward a year. It took the form of a three-stage consultation and took 18 months, before the code was finally published in 2010. Even before that, the government ordered a specific review of corporate governance for financial institutions, which argued in part that bank governance might need to be different from non-financial companies (Walker, 2009).

As Nordberg and McNulty (2013) demonstrate, the major revisions to the code left the core principles largely unaltered, but they did involve a shift in tone. The Cadbury Code (1992) emphasised in its selection of metaphor and other language features the need for structures to provide a foundation for good governance:

> Our proposals aim to strengthen the unitary board system and increase its effectiveness, not to replace it. (Paragraph 1.8)

> The effectiveness of a board is buttressed by its structure and procedures. One aspect of structure is the appointment of committees of the board, such as the audit, remuneration and nomination committees. (Paragraph 4.21)

> Raising standards of corporate governance cannot be achieved by structures and rules alone. They are important because they provide a framework which will encourage and support good governance. (Paragraph 3.13)

The symbolism was quiet, working in the rhetorical background to let its prime audiences of directors and investors understand its purpose: 'buttresses' of structure and procedure 'strengthen' corporate governance, overcoming the weakness which had led to the series of corporate collapses. That it would be a 'framework' told them that there was still much to be filled in. Director and management discretion would be constrained but not eliminated.

That first code did not invent the idea of board committees; they already existed in many companies, partly a mechanism for efficiency, partly through imitating practice that had developed in the US, particularly for committees to consider audit issues. It put committees—for nominating new directors, including the chief executive officer; for remuneration of the executives; and for audit—at the forefront of the code. It structured their practice by giving non-executive directors a prominent role. As we shall see, these structural elements of board design were rather controversial and remained so in the early years.

The 2003 revision to the Combined Code, without changing the structures, shifted the weight of emphasis to director independence. While Cadbury had given special value to the non-executive directors, the experience of corporate collapses abroad—importantly in the US—raised doubts about whether just being non-executive gave enough protection against managerial power. In the worst US collapses, the outside directors were anything but independent. Studies of board interlocks—directors sitting on the boards of companies with directors on the other firm's board—show the presence of cosy relationships, which can impede critical thinking and boardroom challenge (Shipilov, Greve, & Rowley, 2010) and increase executive pay (Hallock, 1997). Some of the evidence of US experience post-Enron suggests board interlocks continue to be a large and even growing part of the corporate landscape (Withers, Kim, & Howard, 2018).

In the UK, a review of the effectiveness of non-executive directors, conducted by the former investment banker Derek Higgs (2003), called for sweeping changes. Unlike the Cadbury Committee, the Higgs Review was directly a government intervention. It urged that all three board committees be controlled by, not just include, non-executive directors who had no ties to management. His recommendations were controversial, as we shall see, and were not incorporated in their entirety in the new Combined Code (FRC, 2003). But non-executives not deemed independent almost vanished from the code. In the Cadbury Code, at least a third of board members were supposed to be non-executive and most of them independent; in 2003, at least half the seats should be held by non-executives, all of whom would be independent. Moreover, in the 2003 code, the chair should meet the standards of independence at the time of appointment. No longer should a CEO 'retire' to the chairmanship.

In 2010, the post-financial crisis code left the Cadbury structures and principles largely intact; the changes not only maintained but also strengthened board independence. But in its diction and tone, the renamed UK Corporate Governance Code (FRC, 2010) also placed greater emphasis on relationships—between directors themselves, and between the board and shareholders. In a new section near the start with the heading 'Comply or Explain', it said:

> The 'comply or explain' approach is the trademark of corporate governance in the UK. It has been in operation since the Code's beginnings and is the foundation of the Code's flexibility. It is strongly supported by both companies and shareholders and has been widely admired and imitated internationally.
>
> The Code is not a rigid set of rules.... ('Comply or Explain,' Paragraphs 1–2)

The alliterations—'foundation ... flexibility', then 'not a rigid set of rules'—build the sense that the structures of 1992 and the independence in 2003 had missed something important. The equivalent section in the Cadbury Code of 1992 is labelled simply 'Compliance', not a ringing call for explanation:

> Raising standards of corporate governance cannot be achieved by structures and rules alone. They are important because they provide a framework which will encourage and support good governance, but what counts is the way in which they are put to use. (Paragraph 3.13)

Cadbury built structures and frameworks and placed the emphasis there, while acknowledging that 'what counts' might lie elsewhere. The 2010 code encourages its principal audiences—directors and investors—to bend the rules and pay more attention to what Cadbury thought 'counts'. This new code was, as Nordberg and McNulty (2013) put it, a recognition as much of the limitations of codification as of its possibilities.

During these major revisions after crises, as well as the other periodic reviews, the key principles and specific recommendations of the code were left largely unchanged. Gradually other recommendations were added, for example, on membership of and attendance at board committees, gender diversity, and board evaluation (Nordberg & Booth, 2019).

These changes added layers of specific measures that required compliance, albeit under the 'comply-or-explain' principle. Governance reports became a regular reporting requirement, and then became longer and more detailed, written increasingly in routine, standardised language, and composed by public relations consultants who wrote the non-financial sections of annual reports.

In the 2010 revision, the principal author, Sir Christopher Hogg, warned against this 'fungus' of 'boiler-plate' (Paragraph 7), urging company chairs to take personal responsibility of the governance report.[2] The danger he saw was that corporate governance might become even more of a 'box-ticking' exercise, and thus detract from the important matter of strengthening board relationships and engaging in serious debates.

The broad agreement on key elements of the code no doubt helped it become institutionalised, that is, accepted as legitimate by most people affected and largely taken for granted. But that does not mean these consultations lacked controversy. Far from it. What was at stake in the debates were issues that might have upset the established order. Much of the custom and practice of boards pre-dated Cadbury. It also threatened to upset existing power structures, including the balance of discretion between corporate management, boards of directors, and shareholders. Codifying new ways of working could open the door to more radical measures—work representation on boards, rights to other constituencies, constraints on direction and managerial discretion, revisions to the nature of the accountability of audit.

This study focuses on three recurrent issues, ones that aroused controversy in 1992 and would not go away: (a) board design, that is, its structure and composition; (b) the resulting effects on the prevalent tone, the custom and practice, that is, the *ethos* of the boardroom; and (c) the nature of compliance. By examining the rhetoric in arguments used by participants in the public consultations that led to the three major versions of the code, we see how the language of the code and the

[2] The 2010 code makes this recommendation. That it was the view of the Sir Christopher comes from a personal conversation with the author of this study undertaken after the code was published. Sir Christopher was chair of the Financial Reporting Council at the time. A former CEO (of Courtaulds plc) and chairman (of Reuters Group plc), he had in 1992 also served as adviser to Sir Adrian Cadbury in the later stages of formulating the first code.

discourse it created reflected the power dynamics in the system of corporate governance. Once its legitimacy was established, the code became an impediment to more radical revisions. Veldman and Willmott (2016, p. 581) discuss this process as one of a 'single loop of reflexivity', but one that has not achieved the 'double loop' that permits more transformational change through 'questioning underlying organization policies and objectives' (Argyris, 1977, p. 117). The debates also demonstrate that the underlying problems persisted, and that alternative approaches resurface with each attempt at revision, to be accommodated, if only in part.

This study develops our understanding of corporate governance in three ways: Historically, it shows how the language of the code developed through the distillation of ideas arising in the consultation process. That process, operating repeatedly in context of political indecision and weakness, led to decisions that favoured central actors at the expense of more peripheral ones with more radical ideas. It shows how, in the centre, institutional investors wrested power from corporations. But it also shows that the processes allowed ideas rejected at one stage to resurface. The code thus was a living document, not a stale, historical artefact. Actors across the spectrum of the investment chain had a stake in its success, and in its perpetuation.

Theoretically, the study shows how logics of action, often voiced but sometimes unstated, create a discourse that valorises certain ideas, which come to be taken for granted as those logics become institutionalised. The consultations led to structures that may blend contesting logics, but by giving legitimacy to alternative discourses through their participation in the process, it left others suspended and held in abeyance, but not vanquished.

Practically, it demonstrates how the process of governing through codes has greater flexibility than legislation or regulation, but also how the institutionalisation of the process can inhibit stronger state intervention or even experimentation with other ways of organising the governance of organisations. The discussion suggests ways in which these lessons may have application beyond the UK and in aspects of organisational life and regulatory process other than in *corporate* governance.

The rest of the study is structured as follows: Chapter 2 provides an overview of the field of corporate governance and provides a framework for thinking about the issues it raises in terms of ethics, the political processes of contestation over power, and how the rules thus devised become institutions.

Chapter 3 examines the context: The historical background and key concepts of corporate governance, including differences in context between the starting point of concern in the US during the Great Depression after the Wall Street Crash of 1929 and the UK, and then extending that to the end of the twentieth century. A detailed look at institutional, market, and political situations in the UK in which the code developed.

Chapter 4 describes institutions, institutional theory, and power: formal and informal institutions, the problem of institutions outliving their usefulness, how institutions disguise power, and how institutional logics illuminate the relationship to power. Less theoretically and philosophically inclined readers may decide to skip this chapter, but they will miss some of the ideas that underpin the later discussion of power relations and impact of the code.

Chapter 5 looks at how the institutional context for corporate governance—especially the battle between the UK and the European Union over company law—created flashpoints for the framers of the first code: the shape of the board of directors (board design), board ethos, and the nature of compliance.

Chapter 6 provides a detailed historical analysis of the inputs of corporations, accountancy bodies and firms, lawyers, investors, and lobbyists over the question of board design, covering 1992 and then the major code revisions in 2003 and 2010, after fresh crises in corporate governance. Chapter 7, in parallel to the previous one, analyses the debates concerning board ethos and compliance.[3]

Chapter 8 provides a critical analysis of what these debates show us about the seat and shift of power between the key actors in the field—corporations, mainstream institutional investors, professional services firms and bodies, and more peripheral voices in the debate. Central actors have embedded their authority over the process, marginalising more peripheral voices but without excluding them, which allows their arguments to resurface in the cycle of recurring code revision. It returns to the framework outlined in Chapter 2 to show how the cycle of ethical choices, political contestation and institutionalisation manifests in the debate over codification.

Chapter 9 offers conclusions about how the code has influenced the practice of corporate governance and how the process of developing the

[3] A description of the research methods and document sampling appears in Appendix A.

code has both built a consensus, a logic of corporate governance while also embedding a lack of experimentation that might have done more to address the underlying problem of corporate collapse. It also notes that participation in the more recent code debates has failed to reflect the shifting patterns of investment in the UK equities market. It discusses how the product of this long debate—the code itself—has changed organisational governance well beyond listed companies and well beyond the UK.

The book closes with an epilogue offering a contemporary postscript, looking at the collapse of Carillion in 2018, a hesitant discussion during the government of Theresa May over having employees on corporate boards, and following her fall from power in 2019 the ongoing debate over regulation of accountancy and corporate governance more widely. It ends with some very initial thoughts on the consequences of the coronavirus pandemic on the economic and corporate governance systems.

References

Argyris, C. (1977). Double loop learning in organizations. *Harvard Business Review, 55*(5), 115–125.

Bank of England. (2015, November). *The failure of HBOS plc*. UK Financial Conduct Authority and Prudential Regulatory Authority report. Retrieved November 19, 2015, from http://www.bankofengland.co.uk/pra/Documents/publications/reports/hbos.pdf.

Cadbury, A. (1992). *The financial aspects of corporate governance*. Retrieved September 1, 2015, from http://www.ecgi.org/codes/documents/cadbury.pdf.

Committee on Corporate Governance. (2000, May). *Combined code: Principles of corporate governance and code of good practice*. UK Financial Services Authority publication for the Committee on Corporate Governance. Retrieved February 10, 2017, from http://www.ecgi.org/codes/documents/combined_code.pdf.

Deakin, S., & Konzelmann, S. J. (2004). Learning from Enron. *Corporate Governance: An International Review, 12*(2), 134–142. https://doi.org/10.1111/j.1467-8683.2004.00352.x.

Elsayed, K. (2007). Does CEO duality really affect corporate performance? *Corporate Governance: An International Review, 15*(6), 1203–1214. https://doi.org/10.1111/j.1467-8683.2007.00641.x.

FRC. (2003). *Combined code on corporate governance*. UK Financial Reporting Council. Retrieved June 20, 2006, from http://www.frc.org.uk/documents/pagemanager/frc/Web%20Optimised%20Combined%20Code%203rd%20proof.pdf.

FRC. (2010). *The UK corporate governance code*. UK Financial Reporting Council. Retrieved May 29, 2010, from http://www.frc.org.uk/documents/pagemanager/Corporate_Governance/UK%20Corp%20Gov%20Code%20June%202010.pdf.

FSA. (2011, December). *The failure of the Royal Bank of Scotland plc*. UK Financial Services Authority report. Retrieved November 19, 2015, from http://www.fsa.gov.uk/pubs/other/rbs.pdf.

Goh, L., & Gupta, A. (2016). Remuneration of non-executive directors: Evidence from the UK. *The British Accounting Review, 48*(3), 379–399. https://doi.org/10.1016/j.bar.2015.05.001.

Hallock, K. F. (1997). Reciprocally interlocking boards of directors and executive compensation. *Journal of Financial & Quantitative Analysis, 32*(3), 331–344.

Higgs, D. (2003). *Review of the role and effectiveness of non-executive directors*. Retrieved October 15, 2006, from http://www.ecgi.org/codes/documents/higgsreport.pdf.

Hodge, C. (2017, February). *Untangling corporate governance*. ICSA Future of Governance series. Retrieved March 6, 2017, from https://www.icsa.org.uk/knowledge/research/the-future-of-governance.

Krause, R., Semadeni, M., & Cannella, A. A. (2014). CEO duality: A review and research agenda. *Journal of Management, 40*(1), 256–286. https://doi.org/10.1177/0149206313503013.

Library of Congress. (2002). *H.R.3763, The Sarbanes-Oxley Act*. Retrieved October 15, 2006, from http://frwebgate.access.gpo.gov/cgi-bin/getdoc.cgi?dbname=107_cong_bills&docid=f:h3763enr.txt.pdf.

Nordberg, D. (2008). Waste makes haste: Sarbanes-Oxley, competitiveness and the subprime crisis. *Journal of Financial Regulation and Compliance, 16*(4), 365–383. https://doi.org/10.1108/13581980810918422.

Nordberg, D., & Booth, R. (2019). Evaluating the effectiveness of corporate boards. *Corporate Governance: The International Journal of Business in Society, 19*(2), 372–387. https://doi.org/10.1108/CG-08-2018-0275.

Nordberg, D., & McNulty, T. (2013). Creating better boards through codification: Possibilities and limitations in UK corporate governance, 1992–2010. *Business History, 55*(3), 348–374. https://doi.org/10.1080/00076791.2012.712964.

Price, M., Harvey, C., Maclean, M., & Campbell, D. (2018). From Cadbury to Kay: Discourse, intertextuality and the evolution of UK corporate governance. *Accounting, Auditing & Accountability Journal, 31*(5), 1542–1562. https://doi.org/10.1108/AAAJ-01-2015-1955.

Roberts, R. (2014, March). The great financial crisis of 1914. *The Alchemist*, Issue 73. Retrieved September 8, 2019, from http://www.lbma.org.uk/assets/blog/alchemist_articles/Alch73Roberts.pdf.
Seidl, D., Sanderson, P., & Roberts, J. (2013). Applying the 'comply-or-explain' principle: Discursive legitimacy tactics with regard to codes of corporate governance. *Journal of Management and Governance, 17*(3), 791–826. https://doi.org/10.1007/s10997-011-9209-y.
Shipilov, A. V., Greve, H. R., & Rowley, T. J. (2010). When do interlocks matter? Institutional logics and the diffusion of multiple corporate governance practices. *Academy of Management Journal, 53*(4), 846–864.
UK Government. (2007, June). *Companies Act 2006: Directors' duties—Ministers' statements*. Retrieved August 5, 2011, from http://www.bis.gov.uk/files/file40139.pdf.
UK Parliament. (2006). *Companies Act*. Retrieved June 20, 2007, from http://www.legislation.gov.uk/ukpga/2006/46/contents.
Veldman, J., & Willmott, H. C. (2016). The cultural grammar of governance: The UK code of corporate governance, reflexivity, and the limits of 'soft' regulation. *Human Relations, 69*(3), 581–603. https://doi.org/10.1177/0018726715593160.
Walker, D. (2009, November 26). *A review of corporate governance in UK banks and other financial industry entities: Final recommendations*. HM Treasury Independent Reviews. Retrieved November 26, 2009, from http://www.hm-treasury.gov.uk/d/walker_review_consultation_160709.pdf.
Withers, M., Kim, J. Y., & Howard, M. (2018). The evolution of the board interlock network following Sarbanes-Oxley. *Social Networks, 52*(1), 56–67. https://doi.org/10.1016/j.socnet.2017.05.005.

CHAPTER 2

The Problems and Remedies in Corporate Governance

Abstract The field of corporate governance has attracted attention from a wide range of disciplines, seeking to diagnose the problems and often to prescribe remedies. This chapter sketches the literature and theoretical perspectives used in the field and outlines a framework for examining the problem at the heart of codes of corporate governance: the work of boards of directors, how it involves ethics and political contests over power, and how they resolve into institutions that inform future decision-making.

Keywords Board of directors · Ethics · Politics · Institutions

Corporate governance is a complex field of study, one with few clear boundaries. Its practice involves a wide range of actors: directors and their advisers, investors and their advisers, regulators, public policymakers, and all the interest groups that seek to advise them. Boards of directors sit at the apex of corporations, where all the strands of the organisation come together. As a result, academic attention to corporate governance has come from a correspondingly wide variety of academic disciplines: accounting, finance, economics, financial economics, law, organisational studies, strategic management, and applied ethics. The breadth of interest has fostered a literature in each and increasingly in studies seeking to create links between the differing perspectives.

D. Nordberg, *The Cadbury Code and Recurrent Crisis*,
https://doi.org/10.1007/978-3-030-55222-0_2

Corporate governance is also a topical field of study, with an impact on both public and business policy. Though it was little discussed before the mid-1970s (Nordberg, 2011), since then corporate governance has rarely been out of the public discourse. Early attention focused on US corporations and in particular on the linked issues of the escalation of executive pay (Balkin & Gomez-Mejia, 1990; Crystal, 1992; Monks & Minow, 1991), the power of social elites (Schmidt, 1977; Useem, 1979) and shareholders' loss of influence (Eisenhardt, 1989; Fama & Jensen, 1983a, 1983b; Jensen & Meckling, 1976).

More recently, other controversies have gained prominence in the public debate. Corporate failures have had an impact on the investment community as a whole but also directly on the pension savings of individuals: let us recall the collapses of the Maxwell enterprises in the early 1990s and Enron a decade later. Moreover, corporate governance failings have been identified as at least in part to blame in the recent threat to the stability of the financial system as a whole (Conyon, Judge, & Useem, 2011; Kirkpatrick, 2009). Corporate governance is not just topical; it is important.

This book is in part a response to both the complexity of the field and its significance. This chapter describes the literature in outline, identifying several recurrent themes concerning the source of the problems in corporate governance and the proposed solutions to them. These diagnoses and remedies point to three underlying ways of conceptualising the field, which form the structure underpinning the individual studies. The rest of the study will use these ideas to analyse the problem that the UK corporate governance code sought to address, and the variety of solutions explored as it came into being and evolved over nearly three decades.

Diagnoses in Corporate Governance

Because interest in the field arose in large part from important corporate failures, much of the literature involves the search for causes and solutions. Empirical studies seek out diagnoses, normative ones advocate remedies, and sometimes the two are linked. The issues can be grouped in at least three broad categories, (a) the work of boards and their relations with managers, (b) the relationship between corporations and investors, and (c) the interaction of corporations with the wider society.

Boards and Management

While corporate governance involves a wide range of actors, much emphasis is placed on the role of boards. Corporate boards have been described as social elites, who meet only episodically and in the setting of fairly large groups, complicating the processes of decision-making (Forbes & Milliken, 1999). In contrast to the high levels of remuneration associated with senior executives of listed companies, directors—in their roles a board members—work for relatively low pay (Zattoni & Cuomo, 2010). Among outside, 'non-executive' directors, many are already powerful, highly paid executives at other corporations or have retired from executive life with comfortable finances. They are motivated less by money than by their personal reputations, a benefit, in theory, to investors who expect these directors to look after shareholder interests, but a condition that may have also a 'dark side' (Fahlenbrach, Low, & Stulz, 2010) for the organisations they serve, when outside directors leave just when their services are most in need. These characteristics suggest that board members are probably strong willed and therefore reluctant to take instructions easily without good reason or without the force of legal sanctions. Indeed, theorists argue that the role of directors is in part to be professionally in disagreement (Amason, 1996; Forbes & Milliken, 1999).

The experience of corporate governance has proved somewhat different. Interest in the field of corporate governance started with concerns over managerial hegemony, a result of the development of what Berle and Means (1932/1991) called the modern corporation, in which remote owners ceded power to the managers of the business. The managerialism identified by Chandler (1977) can run to excess, development of the agency problem (Fama, 1980), often focused on the escalation of executive pay (Bebchuk, Grinstein, & Peyer, 2010; Crystal, 1992). Some studies suggest that boards may be characterised by cronyism (Brick, Palmon, & Wald, 2006), and much of the corporate governance literature has examined potential remedies for these effects in market-based approaches on incentives aligned to shareholder interests (Gomez-Mejia, Tosi, & Hinkin, 1987) and the potential for perverse effects (Bebchuk & Fried, 2003; Lee, 2002).

On this view, corporate governance is a matter of social groups interacting in an economic field. The problems arise from the isolation of boards and the close interaction of boards and managers, which create the risk of expropriation of the company's resources to the private benefit of those in charge. This agency problem may be solved through a combination of economic incentives to give rational actors a reason to work in the shareholders' interests, using a combination of transparency, board structure, and director independence as ways to reduce the impact of isolation. However, it may be argued that the remedies lie not in structures and transparency, but in character, behaviour, and the relationships between the directors (McNulty, Roberts, & Stiles, 2005). These aspects of corporate governance remain relatively underexplored, in part because of the difficulty in studying the practical work of boards.

Corporations and Shareholders

Because an agency problem arises from the separation of ownership and control, the relationship of corporations and shareholders has become an important focus of inquiry. The concentration on shareholder value (Rappaport, 1986) that developed in response to the first wave of interest in the field in the 1970s had at its roots the assumption that the interests of investors comes first, that is, the idea of shareholder primacy (Hansmann & Kraakman, 2004). Empirical studies have explored the impact of shareholders on corporate performance, seeking to determine, for example, whether family control (Bartholomeusz & Tanewski, 2006), blockholders (Laeven & Levine, 2008), dispersed shareholders (Fox & Hamilton, 1994), or other configurations of ownership affect performance or strategic decisions (Daily, Dalton, & Rajagopalan, 2003). While the literature of corporate governance may be dominated by US practice, with its presumption of wide share ownership identified by Berle and Means (1932/1991), questions have arisen whether that depiction is accurate (Holderness, 2009) and how the growth of institutional investment has altered the assumptions of the disempowered shareholder (Edmans, 2009).

Underlying these concerns is a theme of the balance of power between shareholders on the one hand and boards and management on the other, as much as how power is shared between executive and non-executive directors. Rather less attention has been given to another aspect of the problem, the differences between shareholders and how those affect the ability of boards to identify what shareholder interests are, even if they accept the notion of shareholder primacy.

Corporations and Society

The claims of shareholders for primacy are often based not so much on ownership rights as on the notion of residual claims. This approach argues that shareholders are last in line for payment if the corporation fails, so the legitimate focus of boards is to protect shareholder interests (Fama & Jensen, 1983a). This notion has been challenged from a variety of directions, not least from the claim that employees might have based on their firm-specific investments (Brink, 2010), but also paradoxically that primacy might not be in shareholders' interests (Stout, 2011). This thinking is in line with considerations of boards as mediating hierarchies (Blair & Stout, 1999), which recognise the claim of other stakeholders and therefore the role of the corporation in society. Extensions of this approach see corporate governance as linked to the social licence to operate (Graafland, 2002) and a broader social contract (Sacconi, 2006, 2007).

While the literature on corporate social responsibility is in many ways distinct from that on corporate governance, there are overlaps, as when normative approaches based on duty- or rights-based ethics towards stakeholders clash with consequentialist views of utility underpinned by rights-based claims of shareholder primacy. Less well explored are how these interests may be viewed as part of the political contest over corporate resources and how that contest comes to inform the ways in which directors view their roles and choose which course of action to adopt. Such concerns over stakeholder rights form part of the diagnosis of what is wrong in corporate governance and therefore what remedies might need to follow.

Remedies in Corporate Governance

A brief overview of an extensive literature can provide only a glimpse into the range of ideas advanced to diagnose the problems in the field. The range of possible remedies is large as well, and they arise from various perspectives: the character and characteristics of individual actors and the dynamics of their interactions; the legal and regulatory frameworks in which they operate, and the processes or political contestation through which they are formed; the conventions and practices, in particular the codes of practice that guide the decisions of directors. These perspectives have each developed a sizeable literature, drawing upon three interrelated themes.

At the heart of this study is one attempt at finding a remedy—the creation and maintenance of a code of corporate governance in the UK, formed in a crisis and adjusted over time to changing circumstances and in response to further crises. It has proved not only to be remarkably robust, in the sense that its central tenets have held constant, but it has also become remarkably influential, as we shall see, changing practice not only in the UK listed company sector, for which it was devised, but also as a model for corporate governance systems around the world and for governing organisation types far removed from the world of institutional investors and equity capital markets. Its origins and processes fit a framework of governance with three phases, working in iteration, each of which is articulated in facets of the literature of corporate governance.

The Ethics

Let's place ourselves in the boardroom of a corporation. The directors are there to decide crucial, even existential matters affecting the company, its products and customers, the people who create, sell and service them, and the impact the company has on its industry and broader society. The question 'How do they decide?' is in one way or another an ethical one, a thoughtful choice of which rule of judgement applies.[1] It may be a simple question of utility: the greater profits for the least expenditure. It may be a more complex variant, more difficult to calculate: the greatest happiness for the greatest number. It will often invoke questions of rights and duties to those outside the boardroom, or the decision to ignore those concerns. Those decisions might be specific to one set of circumstances or form the basis for a decision-principle to inform a class of decisions. Among the decisions are who to appoint as chief executive officer and who to nominate to join the board and share in future decision-making. These involve questions about the character of the individuals, how they interact with others. The work of the boardroom is, in short, a series of ethical

[1] The idea of thoughtfulness as a characteristic of ethics arises in the distinction Foucault (1990, p. 28) draws between ethics and morality. Morality is 'a set of values and rules of action that are recommended to individuals through the intermediary', whereas the 'ethical subject' decides on a 'mode of being', which 'requires him [sic] to act upon himself, monitor, test, improve'.

choices, dealing with questions of consequences, of duties and rights, and of virtues (Nordberg, 2008).

Some writers on corporate governance (e.g. du Plessis, 2008; Evan & Freeman, 1993; O'Neill, Saunders, & McCarthy, 1989; Orin, 2008) view the field fundamentally as a matter of ethics: The decisions of the directors of corporations that affect the lives of all those with whom it has contact. This approach draws upon themes in leadership, corporate social responsibility, and broader approaches to ethics. But ethical choices of individuals cannot be enacted in a straightforward fashion. Directors work together in a group—the board of directors—creating a need for negotiation of ethical claims, and opening issues of wider negotiation, creating a second avenue of exploration.

The Politics

The ethics of one group of actors—their interests, their rights, their character—will, almost inevitably, conflict with those of others. The solutions they chose to the problems they identify will be contested as the impact of the decision moves outside the boardroom. This implies, almost inevitably, a contestation over power, a political phase to seek solutions that all parties involved can live with. Writers on this theme see corporate governance as a political contest over the resources of the corporation, played out in relationships of power (e.g. Charny, 2004; Gourevitch & Shinn, 2005; Pagano & Volpin, 2005). Indeed, much of the literature examining mechanisms of corporate governance is based on the premise that the solution to the problem lies in changing relationships of power through law or in demonstrating (or not) how such mechanisms improve firm performance (e.g. Daily et al., 2003; Elsayed, 2007; Holm & Schøler, 2010; McKnight & Weir, 2009).

Those contests often involve the struggle between managers, seeking to secure the greatest possible discretion over decisions, and investors, seeking to limit that discretion and keep managers focused on the production of shareholder value. Other actors also play roles in the contest, and all these parties appeal to public policymakers to adjudicate if not the specific claims then at least the rules of the game. The rules provide a third vantage point.

The Institutions

Resolution of such contestation can take a variety of forms, from a simple agreement that then becomes regular practice up to an appeal to a higher authority through law and regulation. The practice of boards is informed by both the formal institutions of law and regulation and the informal ones of custom and practice (Judge, Douglas, & Kutan, 2008; Ocasio & Joseph, 2005; Westphal & Zajac, 1997). Much of the early literature, in particular written from legal or accountancy perspectives, uses approaches focused on compliance and disclosure regulations, for example, and some of the political literature—in particularly those writers working from a path-dependency perspective (Bebchuk & Roe, 1999; Roe, 2003)—see formal institutions as central.

Institutions—the rules of the game, in this case the boardroom game—become maxims for board decision-making, a substitute for thoughtfulness, for individual ethical choices. Compliance suffices, until, for one reason or another, it doesn't.

The board's ethical decisions include the articulation of corporate purpose, the choice of strategy, and the method of its implementation. The resolution of politics creates structures and processes. Once tested those ways of working become institutions, whether of the taken for granted scripts and schemas that sociologists call institutions, the quasi-laws-of-nature in institutional economics, or the legal and regulatory rules seen in institutional studies of law and political science. The framework can be summarised in Fig. 2.1.

Ethical decisions may be taken one decision at a time, by assessing the value of a decision against the aspirations of the board, reflecting a combination of personal value and the interests of shareholders, what ethicists call a task-utilitarian approach, tempered by a view of duties owed to others. Some decisions may be in the form of rules that govern both the immediate decisions and future ones. Rule-based decisions provide a short-cut for future decisions (for a discussion of task- and rule-based ethics, see Nordberg, 2008).

After the contestation with other parties, task-based decisions may become rules, and rules may lead to the creation of structures and processes that provide the mechanisms needed to assess compliance with the rules to the satisfaction of outside parties. These provide the basis for the institutionalisation of those rules. Institutions are the sets of rules that provide legitimacy for decisions; in time they come to be taken

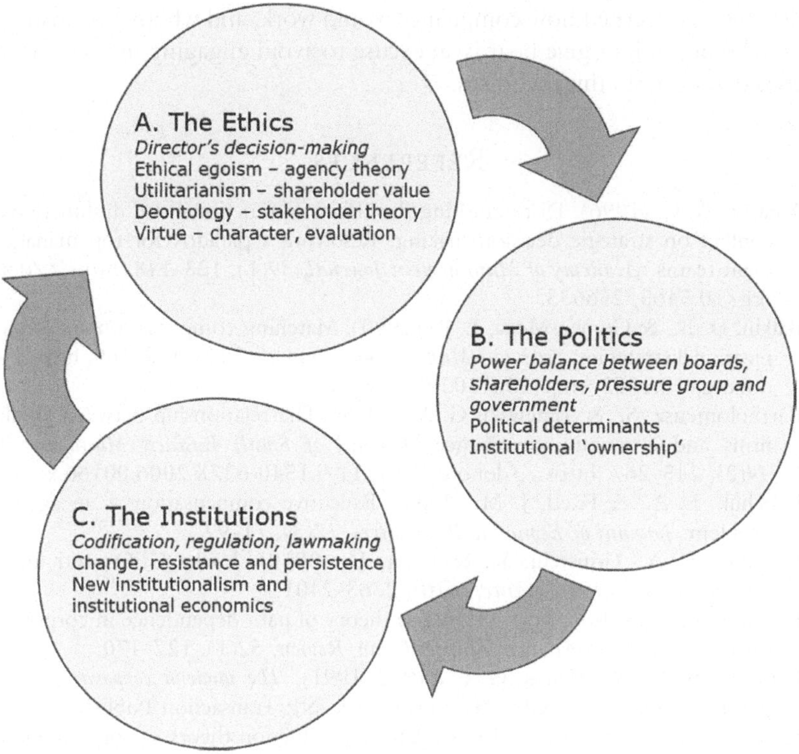

Fig. 2.1 A framework for board decisions

for granted. Adherence to institutional prescriptions, including rule-based ethical frameworks, facilitates decisions, which can then be made largely without considering the consequences. Complying with an institution like a code of conduct makes decision-making easier. Until it doesn't. Defying its prescription pushes ethical boards back to examining—and then explaining—the basis of the choices they make.

Important in the field of corporate governance is an intermediate level of institutional arrangements, not law, not regulation, not driven by economic principles, and not entirely taken for granted. In corporate governance, voluntary codes came to prominence first in the UK and became the benchmark of 'good' governance in many jurisdictions around the world. As we shall see, one of the mechanisms—and central debates—concerned how compliance would work, and whether its institutionalisation might give boards an excuse to avoid engaging in thoughtful consideration of ethical choices.

References

Amason, A. C. (1996). Distinguishing the effects of functional and dysfunctional conflict on strategic decision making: Resolving a paradox for top management teams. *Academy of Management Journal, 39*(1), 123–148. https://doi.org/10.5465/256633.

Balkin, D. B., & Gomez-Mejia, L. R. (1990). Matching compensation and organizational strategies. *Strategic Management Journal, 11*(2), 153–169. https://doi.org/10.1002/smj.4250110207.

Bartholomeusz, S., & Tanewski, G. A. (2006). The relationship between family firms and corporate governance. *Journal of Small Business Management, 44*(2), 245–267. https://doi.org/10.1111/j.1540-627X.2006.00166.x.

Bebchuk, L. A., & Fried, J. M. (2003). Executive compensation as an agency problem. *Journal of Economic Perspectives, 17*(3), 71–92.

Bebchuk, L. A., Grinstein, Y., & Peyer, U. (2010). Lucky CEOs and lucky directors. *Journal of Finance, 65*(6), 2363–2401.

Bebchuk, L. A., & Roe, M. J. (1999). A theory of path dependence in corporate ownership and governance. *Stanford Law Review, 52*(1), 127–170.

Berle, A. A., Jr., & Means, G. C. (1932/1991). *The modern corporation and private property* (Rev. ed.). New Brunswick, NJ: Transaction Publishers.

Blair, M. M., & Stout, L. A. (1999). A team production theory of corporate law. *Virginia Law Review, 85*(2), 247–328.

Brick, I. E., Palmon, O., & Wald, J. K. (2006). CEO compensation, director compensation, and firm performance: Evidence of cronyism? *Journal of Corporate Finance, 12*(3), 403–423.

Brink, A. (2010). Enlightened corporate governance: Specific investments by employees as legitimation for residual claims. *Journal of Business Ethics, 93*(4), 641–651.

Chandler, A. D., Jr. (1977). *The visible hand: The managerial revolution in American business*. Cambridge, MA: Belknap Press.

Charny, D. (2004). The politics of corporate convergence. In J. N. Gordon & M. J. Roe (Eds.), *Convergence and persistence in corporate governance* (pp. 293–309). Cambridge: Cambridge University Press.

Conyon, M., Judge, W. Q., & Useem, M. (2011). Corporate governance and the 2008–09 financial crisis. *Corporate Governance: An International Review, 19*(5), 399–404. https://doi.org/10.1111/j.1467-8683.2011.00879.x.

Crystal, G. S. (1992). *In search of excess: The overcompensation of American executives*. New York: W. W. Norton.

Daily, C. M., Dalton, D. R., & Rajagopalan, N. (2003). Governance through ownership: Centuries of practice, decades of research. *Academy of Management Journal, 46*(2), 151–158.

du Plessis, C. J. A. (2008). Ethical failure under the agency logic. *Group and Organization Management, 33*(6), 781–804. https://doi.org/10.1177/1059601108326802.

Edmans, A. (2009). Blockholder trading, market efficiency, and managerial myopia. *The Journal of Finance, 64*(6), 2481–2513.

Eisenhardt, K. M. (1989). Agency theory: An assessment and review. *Academy of Management Review, 14*(1), 57–74. https://doi.org/10.5465/AMR.1989.4279003.

Elsayed, K. (2007). Does CEO duality really affect corporate performance? *Corporate Governance: An International Review, 15*(6), 1203–1214. https://doi.org/10.1111/j.1467-8683.2007.00641.x.

Evan, W. M., & Freeman, R. E. (1993). A stakeholder theory of the modern corporation: Kantian capitalism. In T. L. Beauchamp & N. E. Bowie (Eds.), *Ethical theory and business* (4th ed., pp. 75–93). Upper Saddle River, NJ: Prentice Hall.

Fahlenbrach, R., Low, A., & Stulz, R. M. (2010). *The dark side of outside directors: Do they quit when they are most needed?* (Fisher College of Business Working Paper 2010-03-007). Retrieved April 28, 2010, from http://ssrn.com/paper=1585192.

Fama, E. F. (1980). Agency problems and the theory of the firm. *Journal of Political Economy, 88*(2), 288–307. https://doi.org/10.1086/260866.

Fama, E. F., & Jensen, M. C. (1983a). Agency problems and residual claims. *Journal of Law and Economics, 26*(2), 327–349. https://doi.org/10.1086/467038.

Fama, E. F., & Jensen, M. C. (1983b). Separation of ownership and control. *Journal of Law and Economics, 23*(2), 301–325. https://doi.org/10.1086/467037.

Forbes, D. P., & Milliken, F. J. (1999). Cognition and corporate governance: Understanding boards of directors as strategic decision-making groups. *Academy of Management Review, 24*(3), 489–505. https://doi.org/10.5465/AMR.1999.2202133.

Foucault, M. (1990). *The history of sexuality* (R. Hurley, Trans. 1st American ed. Vol. 2: Uses of Pleasure). New York: Pantheon Books.

Fox, M. A., & Hamilton, R. T. (1994). Ownership and diversification: Agency theory or stewardship theory. *Journal of Management Studies, 31*(1), 69–81. https://doi.org/10.1111/j.1467-6486.1994.tb00333.x.

Gomez-Mejia, L. R., Tosi, H., & Hinkin, T. (1987). Managerial control, performance, and executive compensation. *Academy of Management Journal, 30*(1), 51–70. https://doi.org/10.2307/255895.

Gourevitch, P. A., & Shinn, J. (2005). *Political power and corporate control: The new global politics of corporate governance*. Princeton, NJ: Princeton University Press.

Graafland, J. J. (2002). Profits and principles: Four perspectives. *Journal of Business Ethics, 35*(4), 293–305. https://doi.org/10.1023/A:1013805111691.

Hansmann, H., & Kraakman, R. H. (2004). The end of history for corporate law. In J. N. Gordon & M. J. Roe (Eds.), *Convergence and persistence in corporate governance* (pp. 33–68). Cambridge: Cambridge University Press.

Holderness, C. G. (2009). The myth of diffuse ownership in the United States. *Review of Financial Studies, 22*(4), 1377–1408. https://doi.org/10.1093/rfs/hhm069.

Holm, C., & Schøler, F. (2010). Reduction of asymmetric information through corporate governance mechanisms—The importance of ownership dispersion and exposure toward the international capital market. *Corporate Governance: An International Review, 18*(1), 32–47.

Jensen, M. C., & Meckling, W. H. (1976). Theory of the firm: Managerial behavior, agency costs and ownership structure. *The Journal of Financial Economics, 3*(4), 305–360. https://doi.org/10.1016/0304-405X(76)90026-X.

Judge, W. Q., Douglas, T. J., & Kutan, A. M. (2008). Institutional antecedents of corporate governance legitimacy. *Journal of Management, 34*(4), 765–785. https://doi.org/10.1177/0149206308318615.

Kirkpatrick, G. (2009). The corporate governance lessons from the financial crisis. *OECD Financial Market Trends*. Retrieved October 26, 2011, from http://www.oecd.org/dataoecd/32/1/42229620.pdf.

Laeven, L., & Levine, R. (2008). Complex ownership structures and corporate valuations. *Review of Financial Studies, 21*(2), 579–604. https://doi.org/10.1093/rfs/hhm068.

Lee, P. (2002). Not badly paid but paid badly. *Corporate Governance: An International Review, 10*(2), 69–75. https://doi.org/10.1111/1467-8683.00270.

McKnight, P. J., & Weir, C. (2009). Agency costs, corporate governance mechanisms and ownership structure in large UK publicly quoted companies: A panel data analysis. *The Quarterly Review of Economics and Finance, 49*(2), 139–158.

McNulty, T., Roberts, J., & Stiles, P. (2005). Undertaking governance reform and research: Further reflections on the Higgs review. *British Journal of Management, 16*(s1), S99–S107.

Monks, R. A. G., & Minow, N. (1991). *Power and accountability*. New York: HarperCollins.

Nordberg, D. (2008). The ethics of corporate governance. *Journal of General Management, 33*(4), 35–52. https://doi.org/10.1177/030630700803300403.

Nordberg, D. (2011). *Corporate governance: Principles and issues*. London: Sage.

Ocasio, W., & Joseph, J. (2005). Cultural adaptation and institutional change: The evolution of vocabularies of corporate governance, 1972–2003. *Poetics, 33*(3–4), 163–178. https://doi.org/10.1016/j.poetic.2005.10.001.

O'Neill, H. M., Saunders, C. B., & McCarthy, A. D. (1989). Board members, corporate social responsiveness and profitability: Are tradeoffs necessary? *Journal of Business Ethics, 8*(5), 353–357.

Orin, R. M. (2008). Ethical guidance and constraint under the Sarbanes-Oxley Act of 2002. *Journal of Accounting, Auditing & Finance, 23*(1), 141–171.

Pagano, M., & Volpin, P. F. (2005). The political economy of corporate governance. *American Economic Review, 95*(4), 1005–1030.

Rappaport, A. (1986). *Creating shareholder value: The new standard for business performance*. New York: Free Press.

Roe, M. J. (2003). *Political determinants of corporate governance: Political context, corporate impact*. Oxford: Oxford University Press.

Sacconi, L. (2006). A social contract account for CSR as extended model of corporate governance (Part I): Rational bargaining and justification. *Journal of Business Ethics, 68*(3), 259–281. https://doi.org/10.1007/s10551-006-9014-8.

Sacconi, L. (2007). A social contract account for CSR as an extended model of corporate governance (II): Compliance, reputation and reciprocity. *Journal of Business Ethics, 75*(1), 77–96.

Schmidt, R. (1977). The board of directors and financial interests. *Academy of Management Journal, 20*(4), 677–682. https://doi.org/10.5465/255366.

Stout, L. A. (2011). *New thinking on shareholder primacy* (UCLA School of Law, Law-Econ Research Paper No. 11–04). Retrieved February 26, 2011, from http://ssrn.com/paper=1763944.

Useem, M. (1979). The social organization of the American business elite and participation of corporation directors in governance of American institutions. *American Sociological Review, 44*, 553–572. https://doi.org/10.2307/2094587.

Westphal, J. D., & Zajac, E. J. (1997). Defections from the inner circle: Social exchange, reciprocity, and the diffusion of board independence in U.S. Corporations. *Administrative Science Quarterly, 42*, 161–183. https://doi.org/10.2307/2393812.

Zattoni, A., & Cuomo, F. (2010). How independent, competent and incentivized should non-executive directors be? An empirical investigation of good governance codes. *British Journal of Management, 21*(1), 63–79. https://doi.org/10.1111/j.1467-8551.2009.00669.x.

CHAPTER 3

Codes and Their Contexts

Abstract The codification of the work of boards marked a major shift of direction in corporate governance. This chapter sets the process in historical context, examining both the market and political settings that pre-dated the Cadbury Code. It shows how those contexts subsequently developed as renewed crises emerged, even as the core tenets of the code persisted.

Keywords Codes of corporate governance · Market developments · Political context

Codes of corporate governance have been in use for long enough now that they have become part of the wallpaper in business practice. So, let's reflect about on the state of play before they become the normative institution they now are.

Boards of directors, even in countries with well-established and well-regulated capital markets, were legally a quasi-sovereign power, even though in practice they often abdicated that role and left executives to decide (MacAvoy, 2003). The absence of oversight of the management of listed companies in the US in 1920 led the scholars Adolf Berle and Gardiner Means to conclude that one of the sources of the Wall Street Crash of 1929 and the ensuing Great Depression of the 1930s was the 'separation of ownership and control', with distant, dispersed shareholders

D. Nordberg, *The Cadbury Code and Recurrent Crisis*,
https://doi.org/10.1007/978-3-030-55222-0_3

unable to influence the decisions that salaried managers made (Berle & Means, 1932/1991). Boards of directors then were largely what today we would call senior management teams.

These arguments contributed to the establishment of the US Securities and Exchange Commission (SEC) in 1934 and led to pressure for boards to become the intermediaries between owners and management. Bringing outsiders, elected by shareholders, into the board marked a partial return to the governance arrangements that had been commonplace in the late nineteenth century, when Wall Street financiers were the large shareholders, and when they personally sat on corporate boards (Perrow, 2002). To be sure, these outside directors did not have the same 'skin in the game' that the financiers once had, but they were a step back in that direction.

Under this logic—institutionalised formally through SEC regulation—outside directors would monitor performance and control the managers, preventing excessive risk-taking and self-interest gouging of corporate resources. This aspect of the role came to be called the 'control' function of corporate boards. But tangible control—tangible power—requires both *information* and *attention*. Regulation could and did require better public disclosure of financial information to the public, but flows of the supplemental, commercially sensitive information that boards needed to monitor performance still lay in the hands of management. Moreover, the attention of these part-time, outside insiders could be directed by controlling the board's agenda.

US practice, then as now, involved so-called 'unitary' boards, in which outside directors, with no executive role, sit with equal legal status to a selection of inside, executive directors. But executives had deeper, more complete information about the business, and were giving the company's business their full attention. These information asymmetries and greater opportunity to use them thus concentrated power in the executive directors. If boards also selected the leading executive as their chair,[1] then control of information, the agenda, and thus director attention could be kept firmly in the hands of senior management. As a remedy for the

[1] This study uses 'chair' as its default label for the leader of the board of directors. In much of the time-period this study examines, chairs of listed companies were all men. The term 'chairman/men' is used when it is the title of the specific person involved and is of course used in direct quotations.

agency problem, boards might reduce the 'separation of ownership and control', but not by much.

Unitary boards play two roles, however (Hillman & Dalziel, 2003). In addition to their formal control over management, they also serve the company's business purpose and its management, informally, as advisers, wise counsel, in setting strategic direction. Outside directors can provide an additional service in providing intelligence of what happens outside the company. They notice things that insiders may overlook.

This 'boundary-spanning', service role can alert managers to changes in the business environment and sometimes provide access to scarce informational resources and business contacts, thus contributing directly to strategic advantage. In comparison to the control function, for a lot of outside directors this 'service' role is, frankly, more fun (Concannon & Nordberg, 2018). These structures and practices also encouraged the appointment of glory-seeking, 'trophy' directors (Dobrzynski, 1996; Fisch, 1997), who bring celebrity but add little to the substance of board work. As the US headed into World War II, control of corporate affairs was, thus, formally in the hands of the board, but informally it resided with the executives.

These US-based directions were different from business practice in much of the rest of the world, where many large businesses were either in the hands of the state or had controlling shareholders in the form of business founders and their families. Control rested with the major shareholders and many of senior managers were themselves owners.

In Britain, things were different. There, families that once led large enterprises as owner-managers shed their control as the Great Depression took hold and as their businesses required outside capital. But families still played a strong role in management, and their personal connections were often good for the business. Operating with unitary boards, these companies suffered less from the separation of ownership and control seen in the US. But deference to family members meant they also benefitted rather less from the use of outside, 'non-executive' directors (Franks, Mayer, & Rossi, 2005).

Following World War II, there was a shift. In the US, corporations that had previously been largely domestic expanded overseas, and their increasing scope led gradually to a concentration of economic power in the hands of executive directors. Strategically unrelated diversification led to the rise of conglomerate corporations, often lacking economies of scale and hence a route to superior performance. But the size of these enterprises seemed to justify higher pay for executives. Because they controlled the boards, executives could, in effect, set their own levels of pay.

By the economic stagnation of the 1970s, these conditions came to a head. Corporate performance faltered even as executive pay rose, and the cost of managerial excess, of the separation of ownership and control again became apparent. The company's *principals*, its shareholders, could not control the board, and the board could not control the managers they hired as the shareholders' *agent*. This 'agency problem' became the focus of academic attention (Fama & Jensen, 1983a, 1983b; Jensen & Meckling, 1976), and over time led to widespread public concern (Crystal, 1992). Moreover, ownership became somewhat more concentrated through the rise of investment in mutual funds and other advances in finance, which gave shareholders a stronger voice in setting the rules of the game.

In Britain, the end of the war brought greater state involvement in the economy and a further loss of family influence and control, but also a rise in institutional investment. When the economic woes of the 1970s hit, the stage was set for change. With the election of a Conservative Party government under Prime Minister Margaret Thatcher came privatisation of major industries and a stronger role in the economy for business decision-making. Institutional investment swelled with a growth of collective investment schemes similar to those in the US, as well as far greater reliance of private pension schemes, rather than the state, for savings. But control of corporations through boards of directors was still largely unchanged: old-school and manager-centric. What was missing was a 'jolt' to de-institutionalise stale, out-of-date practices (Greenwood, Suddaby, & Hinings, 2002).

The context of the code's development can thus be viewed from two levels: the economic and market events that triggered its drafting and major revisions, and the political situation affecting the use of alternative modes of governance in law and regulation.

Economic and Market Triggers and Code Response

The Cadbury Code was born in an emergency: the near-simultaneous collapses of Coloroll, Polly Peck, and Bank of Credit & Commerce International (BCCI). After the committee was empanelled came an even greater shock, the collapse of the two listed companies run by Robert Maxwell. These companies each had chief executives with what the code would call 'unfettered' power. As a remedy, Cadbury emphasised structural reforms to the work of boards of directors, in particular the use of committees for key issues, including audit, and the separation of powers through ending the practice of the duality of the roles of CEO and chair (Bostock, 1995; Doble, 1997). It was a voluntary code, notionally a private-sector initiative without legal authority, to be enforced through scrutiny by institutional investors on the basis of a disclosure of compliance mandated by the London Stock Exchange (Spira & Slinn, 2013).

Following the collapses of many companies outside the UK, most notably Enron and WorldCom in the US, the UK government undertook a major revision of the code, based on the Higgs Review (2003) of the work of outside, non-executive directors. Based on survey evidence and qualitative academic research, Higgs recommended that only non-executives deemed independent of management should sit on board committees. The resulting code, with a distinct change in discourse, added provisions to give independent directors control of board committees for remuneration and audit, as well as stronger influence over nominations of new directors, including the CEO (Nordberg & McNulty, 2013). However, the Financial Reporting Council (FRC), a government-run regulatory of the accountancy profession that administers the code, rejected a recommendation from Higgs that would have forced company chairs not to sit on committees. As with Cadbury, the new Combined Code (FRC, 2003), would be voluntary, subject to what had come to be called the principle of 'comply or explain'.

Between these two versions came two reports, on remuneration policy (Greenbury, 1995) and institutional investors (Hampel, 1998), and then the Turnbull Review (1999) on internal control, leading to the first 'Combined Code' in 1998. These added detail without changing the structural core of the Cadbury recommendations. After the 2003 revision came two more revisions, in 2006 and 2008, which again added provisions without changing its emphasis on board independence.

Then came the financial crisis: Northern Rock suffered a bank run in 2007, requiring nationalisations; then, just after the modest code revision in 2008, both HBOS and Royal Bank of Scotland (RBS) failed. All three—and especially the two large failures—were more severe than past examples, affecting not only those firms, but threatening the financial system (Bank of England, 2015; Bruni & Llewellyn, 2009; FSA, 2011). Moreover, these three banks had complied with the recommendations of the code almost without exception.

After those failures, the government launched a major inquiry into bank governance (Walker, 2009), and the FRC ordered a three-stage consultation on a new version to create a renamed UK Corporate Governance Code (FRC, 2010). Its text put a new emphasis on relationships, between boards and investors, between different investors, and between directors on a board, which Nordberg and McNulty (2013) see as acknowledgement of the limitations of codification as a mechanism of corporate governance: that codes can only achieve so much.

These market and institutional forces pointed to the specific provisions of the code at different phases in its existence. But its broad shape and direction were set by the political conditions at these crucial moments.

The Political Context

In 1991, when the Cadbury Committee was empanelled, the British government itself was teetering on the edge of collapse. Prime Minister John Major had come to power the year before with the implosion of Margaret Thatcher's government. Their Conservative Party was wracked with divisions over its policy on European integration, the Maastricht Treaty on monetary policy, and the opportunities for eastward expansion in the wake of the collapse of the Berlin Wall in 1989 and the Soviet Union in 1991. The West, including Britain, had 'won' the Cold War, and Europe was moving simultaneously towards enlargement and 'ever closer union'. But British Conservatives were battling each other.

In this context, the collapses of several large listed companies, which failed seemingly independently of each other, were a problem too big to ignore but too small to command the attention of the government. Was there something wrong with the system of corporate governance? These problems arose just as the government of John Major faced a mandatory deadline for an election before the middle of 1992, which the opinion polls universally suggested it would lose.

While the government might not be able to legislate changes to company law, something had to be done. That something was the Cadbury Committee. The London Stock Exchange, at that time a self-regulating mutual organisation of market participants, feared for its reputation. The accountancy profession, dominated by a handful of large partnership organisations operating under a regime in which the professions—accountancy, law, medicine—were largely self-regulating, feared for its integrity after failing to spot the warning signs. Together, they called on Sir Adrian Cadbury to lead an inquiry into the 'financial aspects' of corporate governance.

Scion of a family of Quaker businessmen known for their religiously based social responsibility, Sir Adrian was the acceptable face of capitalism, the antithesis of the unacceptable Maxwell. His committee was not directly a government initiative, but instead a market one. Instigated by the London Stock Exchange, it was supported by the Bank of England, keeping government a step removed from the process, though it remained watchful over the process and provided background support (Spira & Slinn, 2013). Then, against expectations, Major's Conservatives won the April 1992 general election, just as the Cadbury Committee was about to publish its draft report.

A decade later, the 2003 code revision came when the Labour Party government under Tony Blair was embroiled in its participation in the US-led invasion of Iraq. Labour had, however, already reformed financial regulation, dismantling self-regulation of accountancy, banking, and the stock market, replacing them with government bodies.

Labour also began a major overhaul of Company Law soon after it won the 1997 election, which pitted the party's left wing, favouring harsh actions to curb corporate interests, against the party's centrist-pragmatist leadership (for background, see Company Law Steering Group, 1999; Sternberg, 2000). Those divisions, including a fight over embedding employee rights in a statutory definition of director duties, led to little progress in legislation, and a new Companies Act would not come into force until 2006. Revision of the corporate governance code was, again, a convenient stopgap.

As the global financial crisis of 2007–2009 took hold and a major recession loomed, Labour began to lose its grip on power, and by 2010 there would be an election that would bring a Conservative-led coalition into power. A modest revision to the corporate governance code occurred, coming into force just before the near collapse of the Royal Bank of Scotland and HBOS, when other major banks also appeared to be on the verge of collapse. With the vacuum in political power, the Labour government empanelled a review of bank governance (Walker, 2009), and the Financial Reporting Council decided to accelerate reconsideration of the corporate governance code. Yet again, the code became a mechanism for action in the face of political paralysis and a convenient alternative to more sweeping reforms.

The macro-political context thus points us to look more closely at the field-level politics of actors in corporate governance. They include corporations and their management and directors, institutional investors, professional organisations including accountants, auditors and law firms, proxy advisors, and those claiming authority based on looking after interests of other 'stakeholders' in corporate activities, and how they contested for control over corporate governance. Before doing so, however, we need to consider field-level theories of institutionalisation and power.

References

Bank of England. (2015, November). *The failure of HBOS plc*. UK Financial Conduct Authority and Prudential Regulatory Authority report. Retrieved November 19, 2015, from http://www.bankofengland.co.uk/pra/Documents/publications/reports/hbos.pdf.

Berle, A. A., Jr., & Means, G. C. (1932/1991). *The modern corporation and private property* (Rev. ed.). New Brunswick, NJ: Transaction Publishers.

Bostock, R. (1995). Company responses to Cadbury. *Corporate Governance: An International Review, 3*(2), 72–77. https://doi.org/10.1111/j.1467-8683.1995.tb00099.x.

Bruni, F., & Llewellyn, D. T. (Eds.). (2009). *The failure of Northern Rock: A multi-dimensional case study* (Vol. 2011). Vienna: SUERF—The European Money and Finance Forum.

Company Law Steering Group. (1999). *Modern company law for a competitive economy: The strategic framework*. Company Law Reform consultation document. Retrieved January 15, 2016, from http://webarchive.nationalarchives.gov.uk/20070603164510/http://www.dti.gov.uk/cld/comlawfw/framewrk.pdf.

Concannon, M., & Nordberg, D. (2018). Boards strategizing in liminal spaces: Process and practice, formal and informal. *European Management Journal, 36*(1), 71–82. https://doi.org/10.1016/j.emj.2017.03.008.

Crystal, G. S. (1992). *In search of excess: The overcompensation of American executives*. New York: W. W. Norton.

Doble, M. (1997). The impact of the Cadbury code on selection of directors and board composition in UK newly-quoted companies, 1990–1994. *Corporate Governance: An International Review, 5*(4), 214–233. https://doi.org/10.1111/1467-8683.00063.

Dobrzynski, J. H. (1996, November 17). Seats on too many boards spell problems for investors. *NYTimes.com*. Retrieved January 7, 2019, from https://www.nytimes.com/1996/11/17/business/seats-on-too-many-boards-spell-problems-for-investors.html.

Fama, E. F., & Jensen, M. C. (1983a). Agency problems and residual claims. *Journal of Law and Economics, 26*(2), 327–349. https://doi.org/10.1086/467038.

Fama, E. F., & Jensen, M. C. (1983b). Separation of ownership and control. *Journal of Law and Economics, 23*(2), 301–325. https://doi.org/10.1086/467037.

Fisch, J. E. (1997). Taking boards seriously. *Cardozo Law Review, 19*(1–2), 265–290.

Franks, J. R., Mayer, C., & Rossi, S. (2005). Spending Less Time with the family: The decline of family ownership in the UK. In R. K. Morck (Ed.), *A history of corporate governance around the world: Family business groups to professional managers* (pp. 581–611). Chicago: University of Chicago Press for NBER.

FRC. (2003). *Combined code on corporate governance*. UK Financial Reporting Council. Retrieved June 20, 2006, from http://www.frc.org.uk/documents/pagemanager/frc/Web%20Optimised%20Combined%20Code%203rd%20proof.pdf.

FRC. (2010). *The UK corporate governance code*. UK Financial Reporting Council. Retrieved May 29, 2010, from http://www.frc.org.uk/documents/pagemanager/Corporate_Governance/UK%20Corp%20Gov%20Code%20June%202010.pdf.

FSA. (2011, December). *The failure of the Royal Bank of Scotland plc*. UK Financial Services Authority report. Retrieved November 19, 2015, from http://www.fsa.gov.uk/pubs/other/rbs.pdf.

Greenbury, R. (1995). *Directors' remuneration: Report of the study group*. European Corporate Governance Institute. Retrieved October 27, 2008, from http://www.ecgi.org/codes/documents/greenbury.pdf.

Greenwood, R., Suddaby, R., & Hinings, C. R. (2002). Theorizing change: The role of professional associations in the transformation of institutionalized fields. *Academy of Management Journal, 45*(1), 58–80. https://doi.org/10.2307/3069285.

Hampel, R. (1998). *Committee of corporate governance—Final report*. Retrieved April 25, 2008, from http://www.ecgi.org/codes/documents/hampel.pdf.

Higgs, D. (2003). *Review of the role and effectiveness of non-executive directors*. Retrieved October 15, 2006, from http://www.ecgi.org/codes/documents/higgsreport.pdf.

Hillman, A. J., & Dalziel, T. (2003). Boards of directors and firm performance: Integrating agency and resource dependence perspectives. *Academy of Management Review, 28*(3), 383–396. https://doi.org/10.5465/amr.2003.10196729.

Jensen, M. C., & Meckling, W. H. (1976). Theory of the firm: Managerial behavior, agency costs and ownership structure. *The Journal of Financial Economics, 3*(4), 305–360. https://doi.org/10.1016/0304-405X(76)90026-X.

MacAvoy, P. (2003). 'Where was the board?' Share price collapse and the governance crisis of 2000–2002. In P. MacAvoy & I. Millstein (Eds.), *The recurrent crisis in corporate governance* (pp. 66–94). Basingstoke: Palgrave Macmillan.

Nordberg, D., & McNulty, T. (2013). Creating better boards through codification: Possibilities and limitations in UK corporate governance, 1992–2010. *Business History, 55*(3), 348–374. https://doi.org/10.1080/00076791.2012.712964.

Perrow, C. (2002). *Organizing America: Wealth, power, and the origins of corporate capitalism*. Princeton, NJ: Princeton University Press.

Spira, L. F., & Slinn, J. (2013). *The Cadbury committee: A history*. Oxford: Oxford University Press.

Sternberg, E. (2000). How the strategic framework for UK company law reform undermines corporate governance. *Hume Papers on Public Policy, 8*(1), 54–69.

Turnbull, N. (1999). *Internal control: Guidance for directors on the combined code*. Retrieved November 15, 2008, from http://www.ecgi.org/codes/documents/turnbul.pdf.

Walker, D. (2009, November 26). *A review of corporate governance in UK banks and other financial industry entities: Final recommendations*. HM Treasury Independent Reviews. Retrieved November 26, 2009, from http://www.hm-treasury.gov.uk/d/walker_review_consultation_160709.pdf.

CHAPTER 4

Institutions, Logics, and Power

Abstract Codes are an important part of the institutional framework that governs the operations of corporations and their boards of directors. This chapter provides a grounding in institutional theory, its emphasis on how structures determine outcomes, and how it can fail to take into account underlying issues of power. It discusses how institutional theorists have turned to two approaches—'logics' and 'work'—to overcome the weakness and account for greater agency of social actors. It argues that a rhetorical view of logics and concern for discourse in work help explain contests over power in codes of conduct and the process of codification.

Keywords Institutional theory · Power · Logics · Work

Institutions are the sets of rules that shape society; institutions enable certain actions and constrain others (DiMaggio & Powell, 1983; North, 1991). Institutionalising rules—where they become taken for granted and acted upon without challenge—tends to favour one configuration of interests over others, cementing power relationships and inhibiting change. Critical scholars have therefore argued that institutional theory is at best partial; it shows why practices persist long after they cease to be useful (Meyer & Rowan, 1977), but glosses over power issues and not explaining change. Because institutional theory seems to remove agency from human and organisational actors or absolve them of blame, it is

D. Nordberg, *The Cadbury Code and Recurrent Crisis*,
https://doi.org/10.1007/978-3-030-55222-0_4

worthy of just two cheers (Kraatz, 2011) or perhaps only one (Willmott, 2015).

To address such shortcomings, two streams of theorising have developed. 'Institutional work' considers how actors create, maintain and disrupt institutions (Lawrence & Suddaby, 2006), while 'institutional logics' explores how sets of rituals, routines, and material practices conflict with each other, unsettling actors who take them for granted (Thornton, Ocasio, & Lounsbury, 2012). Actions are informed, enabled and constrained by higher, institution-level logics, operating in institutional 'orders' (Friedland & Alford, 1991) or 'domains' (Puxty, Willmott, Cooper, & Lowe, 1987). Institutional logics have been defined as 'broad cultural beliefs and rules that structure cognition and fundamentally shape decision making and action in a field' (Marquis & Lounsbury, 2007, p. 799) or the 'principles, practices, and symbols' that shape how reasoning takes place among actors adhering to an institution (Thornton et al., 2012, p. 2). Therefore, 'work' on institutions suggests actors have agency, that is, the ability to influence outcomes. But the argument for 'logics' embracing agency is less clear cut.

That there is a logic to the way organisations and people within them operate is nonetheless a helpful concept. Gendron (2002) uses the term 'logics' in discussing the conflicting commercial and professional imperatives in accountancy. Actors follow these logics consciously, in ways that suggest they are *not* taken for granted; actors have agency and use it deliberately. Similarly, Rahaman, Neu, and Everett (2010) discuss hybridity in social purpose alliances as an attempt to reconcile competing logics consciously, in ways that deliberation and debate.

To find a path from this view of logics to institutions, let us consider the approach of Green, Li, and Nohria (2009), who employ the concept of syllogisms in logic to explain how rules develop from arguments and become embedded in social relations. For a logical argument ('if A and B, then C') to become institutionalised, its premises come to be taken for granted ('if A, then C'). As that process continues, logics can become fully embedded social structures (i.e. just 'C'). Using Toulmin's (2003) nomenclature, the grounds and warrants of arguments come to be accepted as true, making the claims undisputed and seemingly indisputable.[1] In this way, logics can be viewed as thoughtful, political tools of human actors, who use rhetorical mechanisms to convince others to adhere, eventually in less or unthinking ways, to the rules they prescribe.

This dynamic depiction, of logics and their institutionalisation, lets us see how these actors can gain and then sustain power. They create rules by establishing a discourse. Certain actors develop the vocabulary in which debate occurs, the memorable rhetorical devices that build a discourse, and which legitimates the action and then guides and controls other actors (cf. Fairclough, 1992). The initiators, those whose rhetoric shapes the discourse, can exert power over other actors (cf. Dowding, 1991; Morriss, 1995), especially as those others fail to question the logic and gradually come to take its premises for granted.

An alternative theorisation is that of Moore, Tetlock, Tanlu, and Bazerman (2006), who suggest that issues arise and find resolution through the agency of certain actors' rent-seeking activities, which creates a stasis until either their overreaching or a countervailing force undermines it. This 'issue cycle' then repeats. Their approach is couched in economic and political terms, in which these actors pursue their interests, for example, in promoting regulation to their benefit, which they disguise with politically palatable justifications. This approach thus accounts for the exercise of power in rule-setting through rhetoric, in a similar way to what Green et al. (2009) discuss. The latter's account, however, adds a sociological mechanism through which both the initiators and others in the social system come to accept the rhetoric as legitimate, suggesting that persistence can arise even in the face of exogenous shocks.

Following this line of reasoning, initiators can themselves come to adhere to logics in ways that they, too, take them for granted, drawing meaning not from articulation of the logic but instead from its routine, rituals and material practices. Once institutionalised, these logics persist until confronted with a contradiction that forces actors once again to challenge assumptions. That challenge may come about through the 'precipitating jolt' (Greenwood, Suddaby, & Hinings, 2002) that leads actors to question institutionalised arrangements, or through the entrepreneurial actions of a disruptor (DiMaggio, 1988).

[1] Toulmin (2001) also pointed to the need for 'reasonable' argumentation, rather than narrowly rational approaches, owing to the complexity of social relations. For its relevance in corporate governance, see Nordberg (2018).

Douglas and Wildavsky (1982) have suggested that central actors, whose interests are protected by incumbent arrangements, may become complacent. That suggests that those who take the rhetorical sources of their power for granted risk losing it. Meanwhile, those on the periphery can become alarmed by the power central actors exercise. Peripheral actors can instigate change through DiMaggio's (1988) institutional entrepreneurship, which may include importing ideas from adjacent fields (Rao & Giorgi, 2006). However, Greenwood and Suddaby (2006) find that central actors also initiate change, because their greater resources facilitate such boundary-spanning.

With this theoretical framing in mind, we can see the writing of a code of conduct as a contest for power enacted through the rhetoric of a consultation process. The process creates a discourse that informs changes in social practices that become embedded as the logics diffuses through the social system and the questioning of the logic subsides. In the case of UK corporate governance, the actors instigating the code (the Stock Exchange; accountants/auditors) were not those directly controlled by the code (corporations) or those monitoring its implementation and its direct beneficiaries (institutional investors). That is, the instigators held a position at some distance from the locus of the contest, but not at the periphery. Sir Adrian Cadbury decided to focus on managers, the board and their accountability, rather than just the 'financial aspects' associated with the failure of auditors to stop the impending crisis (Spira & Slinn, 2013). Doing so ensured the debate centred on the contest between managers of businesses and investors.

However, the instigators established a principle of regular revision, which provided a mechanism to re-open the debate. It permitted new ideas to surface but also gave previously rejected recipes and logics another hearing. Moreover, and as we shall see, Sir Adrian gave the code a comply or explain regime. He seemed to adopt a pragmatic approach (Dewey, 1929), one that learns from experience and recognises both uncertainty and the prospect of change. In so doing, Cadbury's code institutionalised opportunities for its own de-institutionalisation, opening the code to periodic contestation. We turn next to examine some of the issues that found resolution in the code, but which never quite went away.

References

Dewey, J. (1929). *Experience and nature*. London: George Allen & Unwin.

DiMaggio, P. J. (1988). Interest and agency in institutional theory. In L. G. Zucker (Ed.), *Institutional patterns and culture* (pp. 3–32). Cambridge, MA: Ballinger.

DiMaggio, P. J., & Powell, W. W. (1983). The iron cage revisited: Institutional isomorphism and collective rationality in organizational fields. *American Sociological Review, 48*(2), 147–160.

Douglas, M., & Wildavsky, A. (1982). *Risk and culture: An essay on the selection of technological and environmental dangers*. Berkeley: University of California Press.

Dowding, K. M. (1991). *Rational choice and political power*. Aldershot: Edward Elgar.

Fairclough, N. (1992). *Discourse and social change*. Cambridge: Polity Press.

Friedland, R., & Alford, R. R. (1991). Bringing society back in: Symbols, practices, and institutional contradictions. In W. W. Powell & P. DiMaggio (Eds.), *The new institutionalism in organizational analysis* (pp. 232–263). Chicago: University of Chicago Press.

Gendron, Y. (2002). On the role of the organization in auditors' client-acceptance decisions. *Accounting, Organizations and Society, 27*(7), 659–684. https://doi.org/10.1016/S0361-3682(02)00017-X.

Green, S. E., Jr., Li, Y., & Nohria, N. (2009). Suspended in self-spun webs of significance: A rhetorical model of institutionalization and institutionally embedded agency. *Academy of Management Journal, 52*(1), 11–36. https://doi.org/10.5465/amj.2009.36461725.

Greenwood, R., & Suddaby, R. (2006). Institutional entrepreneurship in mature fields: The Big Five accounting firms. *Academy of Management Journal, 49*(1), 27–48.

Greenwood, R., Suddaby, R., & Hinings, C. R. (2002). Theorizing change: The role of professional associations in the transformation of institutionalized fields. *Academy of Management Journal, 45*(1), 58–80. https://doi.org/10.2307/3069285.

Kraatz, M. S. (2011). Two cheers for institutional work. *Journal of Management Inquiry, 20*(1), 59–61. https://doi.org/10.1177/1056492610387223.

Lawrence, T. B., & Suddaby, R. (2006). Institutions and institutional work. In S. Clegg, C. Hardy, T. B. Lawrence, & W. R. Nord (Eds.), *The Sage handbook of organization studies* (2nd ed., pp. 215–254). London: Sage.

Marquis, C., & Lounsbury, M. (2007). Vive la résistance: Competing logics and the consolidation of U.S. community banking. *Academy of Management Journal, 50*(4), 799–820.

Meyer, J. W., & Rowan, B. (1977). Institutionalized organizations: Formal structure as myth and ceremony. *American Journal of Sociology, 83*(2), 340–363.

Moore, D. A., Tetlock, P. E., Tanlu, L., & Bazerman, M. H. (2006). Conflicts of interest and the case of auditor independence: Moral seduction and strategic issue cycling. *Academy of Management Review, 31*(1), 10–29. https://doi.org/10.5465/AMR.2006.19379621.

Morriss, P. (1995). Book review: Keith M. Dowding, Rational choice and political power, Aldershot, Edward Elgar, 1991, pp. 208. *Utilitas, 7*(1), 181–184. https://doi.org/10.1017/s0953820800001977.

Nordberg, D. (2018). Edging toward 'reasonably' good corporate governance. *Philosophy of Management, 17*(3), 353–371. https://doi.org/10.1007/s40926-017-0083-9.

North, D. C. (1991). Institutions. *Journal of Economic Perspectives, 5*(1), 97–112. https://doi.org/10.1257/jep.5.1.97.

Puxty, A. G., Willmott, H. C., Cooper, D. J., & Lowe, T. (1987). Modes of regulation in advanced capitalism: Locating accountancy in four countries. *Accounting, Organizations and Society, 12*(3), 273–291. https://doi.org/10.1016/0361-3682(87)90041-9.

Rahaman, A., Neu, D., & Everett, J. (2010). Accounting for social-purpose alliances: Confronting the HIV/AIDS pandemic in Africa. *Contemporary Accounting Research, 27*(4), 1093–1129. https://doi.org/10.1111/j.1911-3846.2010.01040.x.

Rao, H., & Giorgi, S. (2006). Code breaking: How entrepreneurs exploit cultural logics to generate institutional change. *Research in Organizational Behavior, 27*, 269–304. https://doi.org/10.1016/S0191-3085(06)27007-2.

Spira, L. F., & Slinn, J. (2013). *The Cadbury committee: A history*. Oxford: Oxford University Press.

Thornton, P. H., Ocasio, W., & Lounsbury, M. (2012). *The institutional logics perspective: A new approach to culture, structure, and process*. Oxford: Oxford University Press.

Toulmin, S. (2001). *Return to reason*. Cambridge, MA: Harvard University Press.

Toulmin, S. (2003). *The uses of argument* (Updated ed.). Cambridge: Cambridge University Press.

Willmott, H. (2015). Why institutional theory cannot be critical. *Journal of Management Inquiry, 24*(1), 105–111. https://doi.org/10.1177/1056492614545306.

CHAPTER 5

Issues Contested in the UK Code

Abstract In creating a new, semi-formal institution, the UK code challenged existing custom and practice. While some of its principles proved relatively unconfrontational, others did not and the debate over them has continued through multiple iterations of the code. This chapter provides the background of three such areas of dispute: the shape of the board of directors, the ethos of the boardroom, and the nature of compliance.

Keywords Contested issues · Board design · Boardroom ethos · Compliance

Subsequent versions of the code would have Cadbury's as a benchmark, but the Cadbury Committee did not start with a blank slate. Custom and practice, what institutional theorists call mimesis (DiMaggio & Powell, 1983), constrained the drafting. However, codifying board practice would immediately establish a 'proto-institution' (Lawrence, Hardy, & Phillips, 2002) that could challenge established practice. Doing so would replace mimetic isomorphism with a normative type. In the debate that developed, two particularly salient contests would emerge: the design of the board and the nature of compliance.

Cadbury's principles have gained wide acceptance. It is now very rare that a UK listed company would place the chair of the board in executive control of day-to-day business decisions. Declaring an end to so-called

D. Nordberg, *The Cadbury Code and Recurrent Crisis*,
https://doi.org/10.1007/978-3-030-55222-0_5

CEO duality—the single person as 'chairman and CEO'—was a crowning achievement of the code, so as to prevent any one person from having 'unfettered' boardroom influence. The code also mandated a minimum number of non-executive directors and urged that most of them were independent of ties to senior management or had business dealings with the company. Research into the effects of both these hallmarks of the code give ambiguous results, in terms of outcomes, measures like profitability or strategic responsiveness. But for many people in corporations, at investment houses, and in the general public, the principle—in ethical terms, the 'duty' of directors—overrides mere 'utility'.

The logic of these touchstones of corporate governance is not only widely accepted now but went largely uncontested during Cadbury's deliberations, or since. But other aspects of the code, and what it meant for board practice, were contested, repeatedly, and in largely the same terms, and with largely the same outcomes. We look now at three of them: board design, the ethos of the boardroom, and the nature of compliance.

Board Design

Boards of British companies were generally ones with a combination of executives and outside, non-executive directors. While case law existed, the Companies Act said little about them and at that time said nothing at all about their duties. Introducing a code at all represented a break with established practice, in which boards of directors, led by top executives, had discretion. The practice was a 'unitary' board design, with collective responsibility of all directors, executives, and outsiders, for any decisions. Company law did not—and still does not—distinguish between these types of directors.

The logic of unitary boards is this: Executives bring their intimate knowledge of operations and markets to the board, while non-executives provide perspective and a degree of detachment to challenge assumptions that a cosy group of executives might develop. The 'controlling' role of directors is balanced by emphasis on the boundary-spanning and resource provision aspects of the 'service' role (Hillman & Dalziel, 2003; Kim, Burns, & Prescott, 2009). The danger in unitary boards is that they may become too friendly, too cohesive, and lack the cognitive conflict necessary to challenge the executives (Forbes & Milliken, 1999). Allowing top management to participate in nominating new directors creates a further danger they will select friendly or lazy directors, or seek out the famous or fashionable as 'trophy directors' (Branson, 2012; Dobrzynski, 1996), in preference to sceptical ones.

This configuration has an analogue in US practice, but it stands in sharp contrast to the two-tier governance common in continental Europe, where a supervisory board, with no executive members, oversees the work of a management board. Theoretically, the issue concerns agency theory, which suggests that managers will exploit their positions of power over firm resources and superior access to information for their own benefit (Fama & Jensen, 1983). The remedies include constraints on executive power through greater accountability and lower information asymmetries through enhanced corporate reporting. The former focuses on board independence, the latter on public disclosure. The argument for a two-tier board design seeks to address both points. First, the upper tier—the supervisory board—has both structural and constitutional power to resist the influence of executive members. Second, as the legally constituted authority for the company's affairs, the supervisory board can command enhanced public disclosure but also full access to commercially sensitive company information.

As this study shows, this issue was hotly debated in 1991–1992, and that in the first debate Cadbury himself was open to alternatives. While victory then went to corporations and mainstream investors, more peripheral actors won concessions that central actors feared would create a two-tier board via the back door. Moreover, the issue never goes to rest. In the next great crisis in the early 2000s, it arose again, only to get pushed back, though with more adaptations. And again, in the wake of the financial crisis, a protracted, three-stage consultation focused on it again, with the same outcome, yet still without the experimentation Cadbury had contemplated.

Boardroom Ethos

In the time before the Cadbury Code, boards were the primary governing structure in UK companies. Companies existed under company law, of course, but the law deliberately pitched at a very high level. It was not until 2006 that law made any attempt to specify the duties of directors. Indeed, companies needed to have only one director, and directors could themselves be companies, which would then nominate human beings as their proxies.[1] This configuration while far from common, arguably extends the limitation of liability of the director-corporation to the function of the director, while in extreme cases—of insolvency or for breach of duty—human directors' liability is unlimited.

What that meant in practice was that directors were subject to appointment by the 'members' of the company—the shareholders, in effect—and then to the articles of association that members had approved. Once appointed they were free to operate pretty much as they chose. Boards were the source of and constraint on the degree of discretion afforded to managers. Boards were largely sovereign. It is easy to understand, therefore, that boards and directors might resist any attempt to specify in code not just the structure and processes of boards but also the behaviour of directors.

The code itself says little about ethos, though its successive authors have used the 'bully pulpit' of its preamble or preface to mount pleas about the prevalent tone of the boardroom and behaviour and relationships within boards and between boards and shareholders. The 1992 Cadbury Code itself is just two pages of text, but the report of the committee's findings runs to more than 80 pages with the aim of showing how the code is 'designed to achieve the necessary high standards of corporate behaviour' (Cadbury, 1992, Section 1.3). 'All directors, therefore, whether or not they have executive responsibilities, have a monitoring role and are responsible for ensuring that the necessary controls over the activities of their companies are in place – and working' Cadbury (1992, Section 1.8). At one level this passage could be seen as just a statement of company law; but law at the time imposed no specific duties on directors.

Before 2003, the code had already added concerns about executive pay and how boards should interact with shareholders. The new Combined Code that year included as an appendix recommendations on board conduct from the Higgs Review (2003) concerning, among other things, the sort of induction that should be provided to new directors,

[1] In 2014, the Conservative-led coalition with the Liberal Democrats mooted ending the practice of 'corporate directors', but the effort was derailed later after the 2015 election yielded a Conservative majority, which then became embroiled in infighting over membership in the European Union.

how company chairs should interact with other directors, and how non-executive directors should question 'intelligently' and listen 'sensitively'. These recommendations are at once common sense and a scolding.

In the 2010 revision of the code, the preface urged that 'boards must think deeply, thoroughly and on a continuing basis, about their overall tasks and the implications of these for the roles of their individual members'. It urged 'frankness and openness of mind' among directors. These, again, are common sense recommendations; that they were mentioned at all carries the sensed that boards had not done so in the run-up to the financial crisis.

Compliance and Enforcement

A third issue that surfaced repeatedly concerned the definition of compliance and the processes of enforcement. While compliance worried many participants in the Cadbury debate, the committee adopted a logic that made the code voluntary: Among the options for complying with the code was a provision that any non-compliance could be accompanied by an explanation.

Nonetheless, the Cadbury Code stipulated a penalty for non-compliance, *in extremis*, delisting from the London Stock Exchange. Punishment presumes enforcement, however, and creates the problem of how to assess whether any explanation of non-compliance failed to reach a subjective and unarticulated standard. The solution was to give that role to institutional investors, who were deemed to have the resources to assess disclosures of financial and managerial performance.

In the 1991–1992 debate, the question of non-compliance caused considerable anxiety among corporations. In subsequent revisions, as we shall see, the concern would shift to how proxy voting services could determine the way investors judged compliance. Yet the provision has had little impact in practice. Even though explanations of non-compliance have been found less than complete (Arcot, Bruno, & Faure-Grimaud, 2010; FRC, 2012; UHY Hacker Young, 2017) and rhetorically more misleading over time (Shrives & Brennan, 2017), companies retained their place on the market. After listing powers passed from the Stock Exchange to government regulators in the early 2000s, the Stock Exchange created a 'premium' category for companies that complied and a lower category for those that didn't. That decision still begged questions about what constitutes compliance and of the quality of explanations.

The Unsettled Debates

These three issues remain controversial, despite more than a quarter of a century of experience and regular consultation and revision. They are not the only challenges the code has faced, but they challenge the premise that codes of conduct suffice in dealing with the issues inherent in the governance of corporate entities, especially those that can pose a systemic risk, nationally and globally, to banking and finance.

Moreover, these issues sparked debate during the consultation processes over the impact the code might have on the functioning of boards themselves. As we shall see, board design was seen as having the potential to change deeply the nature of board interactions, and with it the ethos of directorship. Compliance, too, led to the concern over ethos, as it was an assault on the sovereignty of board decision-making (Nordberg, 2017).

How these solutions arose can be understood in part through the context of development of the code described above. However, the corporate governance literature has had surprisingly little to say about the processes of codification. A welcome addition is the account by Spira and Slinn (2013), who draw upon committee notes and contributions from the consultations Cadbury conducted. They show a jostling among the various actors from the fields of corporations, investors, accountants, advisers, pressure groups, and politicians.

This study employs techniques from the work of Nordberg and McNulty (2013) on the language of the code itself to look in detail at the contributions of individuals and organisations that participated in the consultations that led to the formulation of the code (see Appendix A for an overview of the methods used). It looks behind the scenes at how the code developed over time to show what the actors say during consultations over the code help to surface the underlying logics they seek to embed in the new institution of the code and then defend over time. In so doing, it provides a view of where control over the processes of codification lie, and how the mechanism for regular review holds the promise of future realignment, if not always its fulfilment.

References

Arcot, S., Bruno, V., & Faure-Grimaud, A. (2010). Corporate governance in the UK: Is the comply or explain approach working? *International Review of Law and Economics, 30*(2), 193–201. https://doi.org/10.1016/j.irle.2010.03.002.

Branson, D. M. (2012). Initiatives to place women on corporate boards of directors—A global snapshot. *Journal of Corporation Law, 37*(4), 793–814.

Cadbury, A. (1992). *The financial aspects of corporate governance*. Retrieved September 1, 2015, from http://www.ecgi.org/codes/documents/cadbury.pdf.

DiMaggio, P. J., & Powell, W. W. (1983). The iron cage revisited: Institutional isomorphism and collective rationality in organizational fields. *American Sociological Review, 48*(2), 147–160.

Dobrzynski, J. H. (1996, November 17). Seats on too many boards spell problems for investors. *NYTimes.com*. Retrieved January 7, 2019, from https://www.nytimes.com/1996/11/17/business/seats-on-too-many-boards-spell-problems-for-investors.html.

Fama, E. F., & Jensen, M. C. (1983). Separation of ownership and control. *Journal of Law and Economics, 23*(2), 301–325. https://doi.org/10.1086/467037.

Forbes, D. P., & Milliken, F. J. (1999). Cognition and corporate governance: Understanding boards of directors as strategic decision-making groups. *Academy of Management Review, 24*(3), 489–505. https://doi.org/10.5465/AMR.1999.2202133.

FRC. (2012). *What constitutes an explanation under comply or explain*. UK Financial Reporting Council Research report. Retrieved September 14, 2019, from https://www.frc.org.uk/getattachment/a39aa822-ae3c-4ddf-b869-db8f2ffe1b61/what-constitutes-an-explanation-under-comply-or-exlpain.pdf.

Higgs, D. (2003). *Review of the role and effectiveness of non-executive directors*. Retrieved October 15, 2006, from http://www.ecgi.org/codes/documents/higgsreport.pdf.

Hillman, A. J., & Dalziel, T. (2003). Boards of directors and firm performance: Integrating agency and resource dependence perspectives. *Academy of Management Review, 28*(3), 383–396. https://doi.org/10.5465/amr.2003.10196729.

Kim, B., Burns, M. L., & Prescott, J. E. (2009). The strategic role of the board: The impact of board structure on top management team strategic action capability. *Corporate Governance: An International Review, 17*(6), 728–743.

Lawrence, T. B., Hardy, C., & Phillips, N. (2002). Institutional effects of interorganizational collaboration: The emergence of proto-institutions. *Academy of Management Journal, 45*(1), 281–290.

Nordberg, D. (2017). Board ethos and institutional work: Developing a corporate governance identity through developing the UK code. *Economics and Business Review, 3[17]*(1), 73–96. https://doi.org/10.18559/ebr.2017.1.4.

Nordberg, D., & McNulty, T. (2013). Creating better boards through codification: Possibilities and limitations in UK corporate governance, 1992–2010. *Business History, 55*(3), 348–374. https://doi.org/10.1080/00076791.2012.712964.

Shrives, P. J., & Brennan, N. M. (2017). Explanations for corporate governance non-compliance: A rhetorical analysis. *Critical Perspectives on Accounting, 49,* 31–56. https://doi.org/10.1016/j.cpa.2017.08.003.

Spira, L. F., & Slinn, J. (2013). *The Cadbury committee: A history*. Oxford: Oxford University Press.

UHY Hacker Young. (2017). *Corporate Governance Behaviour Review 2017*. Retrieved September 14, 2019, from https://www.uhy-uk.com/wp-content/uploads/Corporate-Governance-Behaviour-Review-2017.pdf.

CHAPTER 6

Shape of the Board

Abstract The structure of the board of directors has a lot to do with its purpose. The UK has traditionally had a unitary board, with executives and non-executive directors sharing power. Efforts from the European Commission, supported by peripheral actors in the UK, favoured a change to two-tier boards. This chapter analyses in detail how that debate played out during the three major versions of the UK, which arose in response to crises of confidence, when change was possible, when power might have shifted, and when incremental changes occurred.

Keywords Conflict concerning board design · Unitary boards · Two-tier boards · Power in the boardroom

The unitary board has long been a feature of British corporate governance. Nonetheless, a debate emerged in all three episodes when crisis might have provoked institutional change: Should the UK retain its unitary boards or move towards a two-tier board favoured by the European Commission and modelled on Germany? That country's superior economic performance lent cognitive legitimacy (Greenwood, Suddaby,

D. Nordberg, *The Cadbury Code and Recurrent Crisis*,
https://doi.org/10.1007/978-3-030-55222-0_6

& Hinings, 2002) to the logic that two-tier boards are a 'better' governance instrument.[1] As discussed above, unitary boards unite one set of individuals in both (a) the boundary-spanning 'service' activities, facilitating access to scarce external resources; and (b) the performance-monitoring 'control' activities in agency theory. Dual-board, or two-tier systems concentrate 'control' in the entirely non-executive supervisory board, to which the management board reports. The argument also concerned Germany's use of *Mitbestimmung*, or co-determination, giving trade unions a voice in corporate policy.[2]

Board Design in the 1992 Cadbury Debate

The European Commission had long tried to enact a Fifth Company Law Directive, which sought two politically charged measures: the use of two-tier corporate boards, and some form of worker co-determination. The fight lasted for nearly two decades and was resolved only by a decision not to decide (Winter et al., 2002). The third attempt, starting in 1988, faced strong opposition from UK business people and the Conservative Party government of Margaret Thatcher (Montgomery, 1989), and the battle continued even as Cadbury deliberated.

A general election was due by the spring of 1992. Thatcher had been deposed late in 1990 and John Major installed after fractious internal party manoeuvrings. His government was widely expected to lose the election. On matters like company law and workers' rights the opposition Labour Party might well have taken a different stance.

In a meeting in September 1991, Marjorie Mowlam, Labour's top person on 'City' affairs,[3] made clear her party's intention to legislate.

[1] Ironically, the failures of Herstatt Bank in the 1970s, the construction equipment maker IBH and the bank Schröder, Münchmeyer, Hengst in the 1980s, and the metals trading company Metallgesellschaft in the 1990s find surprising little resonance in discussions of corporate governance outside Germany. The first bank failures in the financial crisis of 2007–2009 were in Germany: Industrie-Kredit Bank and Sachsen LB. Both had invested heavily in US subprime mortgage securities. Even more recently, the financial services company Wirecard, after a spectacular rise into the top tier of listed company, underwent an even more spectacular collapse in the early months of 2020.

[2] In contrast, for example, to Dutch or Swiss practice, half the members of German supervisory boards are drawn from the workforce, a feature of German law since the time Bismarck (Fear, 1997). Roe (2003) links its persistence after World War II to acceptance by capital providers in West Germany of the need to shore up support of trade unions against the threat from the Soviet Union.

[3] The 'City' is a widely used nickname for the London financial district.

Sir Adrian Cadbury's notes of the meeting did not mention directly the issue of board design (CAD-01239). Other Labour members, however, sought two-tier boards in submissions to the committee's deliberations (CAD-01145, CAD-01148), themes subsequently articulated in articles for academic journals (Cousins & Sikka, 1993; Mitchell & Sikka, 1993).

Even after the election in April 1992 unexpectedly gave the Conservatives another term in power, the Liberal Democrats' response to the draft code (CAD-02443) urged two-tier boards with employee representation on the lower tier, management board, and that worker votes be counted alongside shareholder votes at the annual meeting.

That was an extreme position from a somewhat peripheral voice; the Liberal Democrats were unlikely to gain power. But the archive suggests sympathy for the topic within the committee. Jonathan Charkham, the Bank of England's adviser to the committee, wrote to Cadbury during comment period on the draft. He urged Sir Adrian to assess a proposal from two contributors[4] who argued that giving specific powers to non-executives would be to move 'three-quarters of the way to a two-tier board'. He continued:

> There is much logic in what they propose but I have no doubt that it would arouse the fiercest wrath among our critics who can see only too clearly this kind of development coming and are thoroughly scared of real accountability. (CAD-01073)

Here Charkham identifies with Sir Adrian and declares a unity of purpose in resisting 'our critics'. That those critics see 'only too clearly' suggests regret that the process is so transparent.

This note shows an important voice arguing for radical change to achieve 'real accountability'. Indeed, two years after the code was published, when the committee was conducting its first follow-up review, Sir Adrian Cadbury sought legal clarification from the Department of Trade and Industry (DTI), an indication he considered the issue important. Nigel Peace, the DTI official who had served as secretary to the

[4] The 'Merrett-Sykes' paper Charkham refers to is not recorded in the Cadbury Archive, although Alan Sykes, managing director of Consolidated Gold Fields, mentions it in a separate comment on the draft report (CAD-02141). Anthony Merrett, a London Business School professor, and Sykes made a second proposal concerning the accountability of auditors (CAD-02185).

Cadbury Committee, responded that law did not prohibit two-tier boards (CAD-01363).[5]

Shortly after Major's surprise victory, Cadbury published a draft code in May 1992, and his committee undertook a more formal consultation to guide the final code, published that December. In reviewing responses to the draft, the committee took special note of three categories of respondents: companies, investors, and accountancy, an analytic device followed here. They were summarised for committee members in CAD-02255, CAC-02257, CAD-02259, respectively.

Investor Reactions

Fund management organisations, in the main, wrote dispassionately but expressed concern about steps that might split corporate boards into opposing camps of executives and non-executives. One contributor saw something 'dangerous' in the draft, but 'in one or two places'; another said the draft makes 'too great a distinction' but adds director interests are only 'somehow opposed'; a comment on the 'different roles but equal responsibilities' accepted division even as it affirms unity; changes 'may bring a distinction' between classes of directors; the report 'undermines' the concept of the unitary board, but only 'to some extent'. (Fuller context of these remarks appears in Table 6.1.)

An important voice was the Association of British Insurers (ABI), whose membership invested in assets amounting to about 25% of the value of the stock market at the time. Many were listed companies, with interests straddling the investor/corporation divide. The ABI eschewed emotive language on this issue, except for the ambiguously placed word 'disappointing' in the following passage:

> It is perhaps disappointing that there are some who clearly feel that the recommendations undermine the concept of the unitary board, and it might be helpful if the final report emphasised rather more forcefully the support for the unitary board. (ABI, CAD-02467)

At first its disappointment seems to be with the 'some' who criticise the draft report, suggested by the proximity of the two words. But the ABI is

[5] That 1994 review concluded that no changes were needed to the code itself, and nothing more was published.

Table 6.1 Responses of investors to Cadbury draft on board design

Source	*Comment*
Postel Investment Management[a] (CAD-02195)	... the report in one or two places comes dangerously close to undermining the concept of the unitary board
Institutional Fund Managers Association (CAD-02397)	The Report draws too great a distinction between the responsibilities of executive and non-executive directors and could be taken to imply that their interests are somehow opposed. We believe that the Code should place greater emphasis on the need for each director to recognise his responsibility for corporate governance, however the Board is constituted, and for the Board as a whole to recognise its responsibility and that of each of its members
Legal & General (CAD-02353)	We are however concerned that Board balance between executive and non-executive should not be translated into a separation into supervisory and non supervisory functions with the two-tier implication that that would suggest. We see the directors as having different roles but equal responsibilities, with all of them ultimately being responsible to those who elect them—the shareholders
British Rail Pension Fund (CAD-02453)	The additional duties proposed for non-executive directors (together with the previously mentioned head of non-executives) may bring a division into the board if non-executives are to take on a more supervisory role. It is probably more important for companies to describe their internal monitoring procedures and formally report on their operation in the annual report than for a general duty to monitor being ascribed to particular members of a unitary board

(continued)

Table 6.1 (continued)

Source	*Comment*
National Association of Pension Funds (CAD-02449)	So far as reporting to shareholders is concerned, your suggestion that the chairman of the remuneration committee be responsible for answering questions at the Annual General Meeting may well undermine, to some extent, the concept of the unitary board

[a]Postel was reincorporated as Hermes Investment Management in 1995. Through changes in management it has continued to be a strong voice in the corporate governance and investor stewardship debates

not in substance disappointed with those who defend the unitary boards. It is disappointed, rather, with Cadbury for not being more firmly in favour of them, though that point comes clear only after the friendly offer of something 'helpful'. The word order and diction accommodate sensitivities to criticism on this point. That this voice needed to be accommodated is clear from the committee's minutes (e.g. CAD-01303).

The Pensions Investment Research Consultants (PIRC), a proxy voting advisory firm representing mainly local authority pension plans, took a stronger line than mainstream investors in favour of unitary boards, but with a different aim:

> At present many companies insulate some or all of the executive directors from the need to retire and seek election by shareholders. We think this is a serious infringement of shareholder rights and reduces directors' accountability. It also strikes at the heart of the unitary board in which all directors are equally accountable under law. (PIRC[6])

These sentences make clear that PIRC seeks to increase accountability by making executive and non-executive directors face re-election

[6]The PIRC submission itself is not recorded in the Cadbury Archive, but the firm provided a late draft of the document for this study, which is quoted here. The Cadbury Committee's summary of investor reactions cites long passages from the PIRC submission on other matters but only notes that PIRC supported a unitary board. It does not quote this passage.

more frequently. It seeks board unity to increase investor control, not boardroom cooperation.

Accountancy Reactions

Generally, though not entirely, the accountants' contributions on board design objected to the draft and defended the corporate status quo. The first two of the responses in Table 6.2 ameliorate the critique with phrases like 'tends to imply' and 'understand and accept'. But the more forceful language ('unrealistic', 'inimical') of the third quote, from Ernst & Young, suggests that feelings were strong.

In a handwritten note (CAD-02475), Sir Adrian commented that he was 'a bit shaken by the Ernst & Young demolition job'.[7]

The Institute of Chartered Accountants in England and Wales (ICAEW), an important professional association whose members included many company chairs and finance directors, responded to the draft more gently than the accountancy firms themselves:

> Many have commented, too, that the report appears to recommend structures and systems which bring about the existence of something close to a two-tier board, in everything but name. The recommendation in favour of a leader for the independent element on the board, where the chairman and chief executive role is combined, and for the use of outside advisers by non-executives are examples in support of this perception. We believe that the truth or otherwise of this assessment should be more fully addressed in the final report and that it would be valuable if a discussion of the comparative merits of unitary and two-tier boards in the UK environment could be included, additionally. We do not, incidentally, favour the appointment of a leader for the non-executive directors. (ICAEW, CAD-02181)

The mild phrasing of 'it would be valuable' can be read as a quiet taunt to the Cadbury Committee to justify its position; the word 'incidentally' undermines with irony its neutral reference to the idea of a leader of the non-executives.[8]

[7] The comment referred to the E&Y submission in general, which was also critical of the report in other matters.

[8] For a wry look at the use of euphemisms in British speech, including 'incidentally', see *Economist* (2011).

Table 6.2 Accountants' responses to Cadbury draft on board design

Source	*Comment*
Coopers & Lybrand (CAD-02363)	… the language of the draft report as it stands tends to imply a sharper division between the roles of non-executives and executives than the Committee probably intends. We do not believe there is a satisfactory half way house between the two-tier board and the collegiate board
Pannell Kerr Forster (CAD-02373)	We understand and accept that there is a need for a division of responsibilities within a board and that no large listed company should be capable of being dominated by one individual but we are concerned about the apparent belief that within a board there should be two leaders. We feel very strongly that the duty of the Board (within the constraints of the law) as a whole is to create wealth for the investors. The Board has, therefore, to work as a team, and not to be put in a position where half the Board's main purpose appears to be to police the activities of the other half. We are concerned that whilst the report makes this point … the overall impression of the report, because it deals with controls is one where the vision of the non-executive is that he is there to dismiss the chief executive should this prove necessary rather than provide positive input to the future direction and success of the company. We believe non-executive directors have an important role to play in bringing their broader experience to bear on the board's discussions
Ernst & Young (CAD-02447)	We acknowledge the important contribution which non-executive directors can and should make in this direction but believe that the Committee's expectations of non-executive directors are unrealistic. We also believe that certain aspects of the role which the Committee proposes for non-executive directors are inimical to the concept of the unitary board…. The Committee's proposals would create a two-tier board within the legal structure of a unitary board. We do not regard this as tenable

Corporate Reactions

Corporate critiques were unequivocal in advocating a unitary board and opposing European approaches. Two selected for special mention in the summary document circulated to the full committee (CAD-02255) were these:

> This risks appearing to encourage a two tier board system, and detracts from the fundamental concept of collective board responsibility. Any change in this approach should be statutory. Assuming the Committee supports the UK's unitary system, it should explicitly state this, and the reasons why it prefers this system. (Sir Patrick Sheehy, chairman of British American Tobacco[9])

> The whole thrust of the report is to retain the unitary board but to attempt to engraft a two-tier structure on to it. This is not a workable arrangement. (The General Electric Co. plc; in the summary but also in CAD-02115)

That summary seems sanitised, leaving out some of the stronger sentiments received from the corporate side, excluding ones using the emotive words 'danger', 'resist', 'erode', 'poachers', and 'sham', nor an appeal to more rationalist considerations (from Sir Adrian's former family chocolate company) concerning possible loss of 'commercial advantage'. The remarks are summarised in Table 6.3.

Perhaps the most forceful statement came not from a submission to the committee, but instead an opinion column published in the *Financial Times* newspaper, written by Sir Owen Green, chairman of BTR and an emblematic executive of the era.[10] The article was provocatively titled 'Why Cadbury leaves a bitter taste'. He criticised many aspects of the draft report, including the idea of a 'leader' of the non-executives, and asserted that

> A more divisive aspect … is the way it strikes at the heart of the unitary board. It begins by restating the legal position that all directors are equally responsible for the board's decisions. But the committee immediately

[9] Sheehy's submission itself is not recorded in the Cadbury Archive; this excerpt comes from the committee's summary CAD-02255.

[10] The respect Green achieved is made clear in a case study on his long career at BTR. See Kerr (2006).

Table 6.3 Corporate reaction to Cadbury draft on board design

Source	*Comment*
Lord Tombs, chairman, Rolls-Royce plc (CAD-02377)	In our view distinctions between the responsibilities of executive and non-executive directors, save in relation to remuneration, are both divisive and, for example, in the case of decision-making through a two-tier board, a sham
Confederation of British Industry (CAD-02349)	In that setting it is for the board to distribute functions to its members; attempts to reserve tasks as a rule to one class of directors will create the danger of opening the way to a two-tier system.... We oppose the words 'monitor the executive management' as imparting a supervisory role inappropriate to a unitary board
Institute of Directors (CAD-02423)	While the presence of such a system of checks and balances is an integral element of effective corporate governance, it should no way be allowed to erode the principle of a unitary board
J.F. Mahony, Group Finance Director and Vice-Chairman, Ladbroke Group (CAD-02441)	I would resist any movement towards a two-tier system. I believe that paragraph 4.3 is unhelpful as the role of the non-executive directors outlined in it appears to conflict with the principle of a unitary board in so far as it implies that the purpose of the non-executive directors is to monitor the performance of the board. In this context, the non-executive directors must be monitoring the performance of the executive members of the board, not the board as a whole. The draft report should be amended to make it clear that the principle of a unitary board is upheld in all respects

Source	*Comment*
Alick Rankin, Chairman, Scottish & Newcastle (CAD-02455)	The code, as proposed, appears to identify non-executive directors as 'the gamekeepers' and executives as 'the poachers'. Clearly, this must be quite wrong. It is both divisive and intrusive and damaging to the positive partnership spirit essential in a unitary board. Non-executives have a strong requirement to encourage, to support, and to enthuse—this concept is lacking and severely threatened by the proposals
Peter Jinks, Company Secretary, Cadbury-Schweppes (CAD-02385)	The emphasis on more involvement and accountability of Non-Executive Directors emerging from Corporate Governance must not result in or encourage two-tier Boards, which would be of considerable commercial disadvantage to the company and its investors

> reveals its view of the real purpose of non-executive directors. They are there to monitor the performance of the board (including themselves?) and that of the chief executive. (Green, 1992)

The phrase 'reveals its real purpose' signals a conspiracy exposed, while 'divisive' warns of adverse consequences and 'strikes at the heart' points metaphorically at the murderous intent of those advocating change in the British way of organising boards. The forcefulness of its sentiment and the impact of its argument is indicated by how Green's column was quoted in the committee's summary of contributions, in notes between committee staff, and by letters favourably citing Green's remarks.

Support for Two-Tier Boards

Only a few voices supported the idea of two-tier boards, none with the fervour of the Liberal Democrats. The accountancy firm Arthur Andersen, in a detailed and closely argued analysis, said the committee had paid insufficient attention to what it termed the three roles of boards: supervision, control, and management:

> We believe the Report should be more forthright with respect to the supervisory function of the board. It should clarify the objectives and procedures that fall within the supervisory function and recommend that in all circumstances, the supervisory role should be led by a specific non-executive director.
>
> The Report is predicated on the view that the unitary system is appropriate and the unitary board is itself capable of fulfilling the supervisory function. While we accept that the recommendations in the Report will facilitate supervision, it is disappointing that the Report does not discuss the advantages and disadvantages of alternative forms of governance and encourage experimentation. (Arthur Andersen, CAD-02361)

While emphasising 'supervision', the term used for the upper board in a two-tier system, this language falls short of advocacy of European-style boards. The phrase 'predicated on the view' embeds less critique than other expressions of similar content might. But scepticism echoes in the use of 'itself', an otherwise redundant reflexive, as well as in the 'disappointing' choice not to 'encourage experimentation'.

That Arthur Andersen would encourage experiments suggests a position more nearly aligned with concerns of peripheral players about the need for radical change in board design than with actors at the core of the debate or some other intermediaries.[11] The committee's summary (CAD-02259) quoted the Arthur Andersen view at far greater length than those from other accountancy firms. Sir Adrian Cadbury made the notation 'experimentation' alongside 'unitary board' in his handwritten aide-memoire concerning possible revisions to the draft (CAD-01267), suggesting he took these comments seriously.

Most of these texts involve assertions of unspecified virtues of unitary boards and warnings of unspecified dangers in two-tier boards (see Tables 6.1 and 6.3). A subtext came to the surface, however, in several contributions. Richard Lloyd, chairman of Vickers, argued that UK board practice was 'more genuinely unitary in its nature' than what happened in the US or Canada (CAD-01357). J. B. H. Jackson, a self-described 'professional chairman', worried about importing US practice. Sir Owen Green (1992) was more scathing, attacking the idea that an audit committee should be entirely composed of non-executives as the 'least meritorious' in the draft, 'notwithstanding the practice in the US'. He then added venom: 'The arrogance of this imported proposal is communicated through the committee's own words' as the draft proposes limits to auditors' responsibility while it 'blandly describes the unlimited liability of the board'.

The foreignness of this element of board design perceived in the Cadbury draft came in complaints from several others about 'continental' or 'German' practices, as well as some oblique and occasionally direct references to European legislation (e.g. Confederation of British Industry, CAD-02349). Ernst & Young linked the two themes in warning that the 'failure to implement a more effective regulatory regime in the UK now may well deprive the UK of the ability to influence future proposals which, we believe, will emerge from the European Commission for a European Securities and Exchange Commission' (CAD-02447), a contribution noted in the committee summary as well (CAD-02259).

The 'precipitating jolt' (Greenwood et al., 2002) the UK system received from the failures of Polly Peck, BCCI, and especially the Maxwell

[11] Arthur Andersen was at the time a highly respected voice in the accountancy profession. Its disintegration a decade later after the collapse of clients Enron, WorldCom and others may be traced in part to what we might term governance 'experimentation', but not perhaps experiments in enhanced supervision.

companies[12] forced a debate over the appropriateness of an aspect of corporate governance that industry had long defended. Opposition was based on economic and political considerations but especially on social aspects of board dynamics. The voices from the twin centres of the debate—corporations and large investors—as well as much of the intermediaries argued with varying degrees of force against foreign encroachment in the issue of board design, even though the Cadbury draft report did not explicitly advocate either a German-style supervisory board or an American-style board overwhelmingly populated with outside directors. The strength of opposition is evident in the language of these contributions. Several complained that the changes sought by the draft report would demand much effort from well-governed companies and fail to address the rogues. Green's column in the FT put it this way:

> The report's subliminal message is of the need for total integrity and a healthy objectivity in company affairs. This is strongly to be supported. But the need for a code in addition to existing rules and regulations is doubtful – as is its likely effectiveness in reducing the relatively few instances of misbehaviour. (Green, 1992)

His use of 'subliminal message' evokes symbolically the spectre of manipulative advertising techniques, which had entered public and academic discourse over in previous decades through critiques of technologies to project images interstitially in television signals. Although Green endorses the message, he opposes the medium of its delivery.

In his briefing to the committee about feedback on the draft, Sir Adrian worried about the tone: 'We are said to be "long on accountability and short on drive and efficiency" and to take a negative view of governance'; the code risked 'dividing the board'. The first part of these comments highlights the draft's emphasis on control, rather than service, as the function of corporate governance; dividing the board would divide those functions. He then added remarks that imply the code could damage the unity of a board with a weak chair:

[12] Sir Adrian Cadbury's notes to the committee considering the responses to the draft (CAD-01265) speak of recommendations needing to pass the 'Maxwell test', so called because Robert Maxwell would have signed off his companies as having complied with the code, and neither his directors nor auditors would have challenged that view.

> Do we stay with these? Minor changes ... are no problem. I accept that there is a fundamental issue here and that there could come a point when logic would point to a two-tier board. I do not believe we are at that point yet, (although those who advocate distinct legal duties for ned's[13] would pass it), and that the unity of boards need not be undermined by our proposals, given a competent chairman. (Sir Adrian Cadbury, CAD-01265)

The tone of the code changed in response to the comments and criticism, but these notes from the Cadbury archive suggest the issue was still alive under the surface, even after the final version's support for the unitary board. That Sir Adrian thought 'there could come a point when logic would point to a two-tier board' suggests that the issue was still open, even though hostility had closed it, for now.

Board Design in the 2003, Post-Higgs Debate

With the collapse of Enron, WorldCom and many other corporations in the opening years of the millennium, and the implosion of accountants Arthur Andersen, the Labour government in the UK felt something more had to be done. It commissioned a major study of corporate boards, especially the role of non-executive directors.

In the covering letter to his report for the Department of Trade and Industry, Derek Higgs wrote: 'The brittleness and rigidity of legislation cannot dictate the behaviour, or foster the trust, I believe is fundamental to the effective unitary board and to superior corporate performance' (Higgs, 2003). Moreover, he expressed the view that the 'architecture' of corporate governance, defined as structure and processes inside companies, 'in itself does not deliver good outcomes' (Higgs, 2003, Paragraph 1.3). Yet his 53 recommendations, summarised at the beginning of the document, dealt overwhelmingly with 'architecture', the externally verifiable structures. These proposals revived concerns about two-tier boards and dominated the consultation the Financial Reporting Council held to translate those recommendations into the text of a new Combined Code.

The passage from Higgs quoted above considers a unitary board to be an implicit good, and in one of the introductory paragraphs he elaborates that view:

[13] ned's (lower case) is Sir Adrian's personal short notation for non-executive directors.

> Some have argued that the increasing complexity of business life – whether globalisation or fast changing product and capital markets – is such that the whole structure of the board needs to be re-considered. But the majority view, which I share, sees considerable benefits continuing to flow from the unitary approach. (Higgs, 2003, Paragraph 1.7)

As if to emphasise that point, he later adds:

> Increasing the effectiveness of non-executive directors, while preserving the benefits of the unitary board, is a principal objective of the Review.... In contrast, the European system of corporate governance typically separates legal responsibility for running the company between a management and a supervisory board. In the US, the board is composed largely of non-executive ('outside') directors with only a few executives. Evidence collected during the Review has not convinced me of the merits of moving away from the unitary board structure in the UK. (Higgs, 2003, Paragraphs 4.2, 4.3)

This language shows, however, that the debate concerning board design was not over. The uses of 'unitary' here are defensive: the 'whole structure' needs to be reviewed; that he is 'not convinced' about two-tier boards leaves this issue open in general, just closed for the moment. That he shares the 'majority' view acknowledges the legitimacy of the minority. He has considered other systems ('European' and US), concluding that the evidence in their favour is not convincing. But its subtext further legitimates those views.

Evidence in favour of the UK system is not mentioned, an indication that he and the respondents to his consultation and research studies took those advantages for granted, but the word 'unitary' does not appear in Higgs's proposed text of a revised Combined Code. Whether intended or not, taken together these uses and omissions seemed to give respondents reasons to think Higgs had taken a position somewhat short of a ringing endorsement of the unitary boards.

The FRC used the Higgs Review and its proposed code changes as the basis to conduct only a light-touch, 'fatal flaws only' consultation for a new version of the code. The sharply critical reaction it received came as a surprise (Nicholson, 2008). The Association of British Insurers, a mainstream investor voice, saw a 'potential danger to the unitary board' if the code had a 'formal requirement' that non-executive directors meet periodically without the executives or the chair present (April 2003).[14] In a literal sense, this is arguing against a case Higgs did not make. Higgs did not *require* such a move; the text of his draft was that of recommendation: 'should meet regularly as a group without the executives present and at least once a year without the chairman present' (Higgs, 2003, Provision A.1.5), where 'should' also sits underneath the code's 'comply-or-explain' principle.

The CBI, representing large corporations, used more forceful language to make a similar point. It expressed 'deep reservations' about provisions that 'concern or affect the chairman', whose role is 'pivotal in the UK's tried and tested unitary board system'. The choice of 'pivotal' here echoes with irony Higgs's language (Higgs, 2003, Paragraph 5.1), seeking to reverse his intent. The CBI's next sentence elaborates this concern relating it to separate meetings of non-executives, suggesting the provision 'could be misunderstood and could lead to a two-tier board in practice' (16 April 2003). The use of 'could be misunderstood' is an example of language aimed at repairing unintended damage in drafting to maintain the core values of the code. The word might be read as a diplomatic way of disrupting a feared change in direction. As in the ABI submission, the value in a unitary board does not receive, or seem to require, explanation or articulation; neither does the 'danger' or 'risk' in a two-tier board.

Sentiment on this point was even stronger among company chairs. For example, Sir Brian Moffat, chair of the steelmaker Corus, wrote (20 March 2003) in his capacity as senior independent director of the banking group HSBC not to the FRC, but to its perceived political master: Secretary of State for Trade and Industry Patricia Hewitt.

He began with a not-too-subtle attack on what he saw as an attempt to divide the board: He stated his discomfort about writing separately from his fellow directors, lest it be viewed as 'undermining the unitary board principle or the Chairman's position'. Such was the 'strength of feeling and support in the Board' that he needed to add his voice to that of the HSBC chairman, Sir John Bond, who also wrote to Hewitt on this point (17 March 2003), and later to the FRC (11 April 2003). Moffat wrote under Corus letterhead, making a symbolic further claim of

[14] Owing to the circumstances concerning the source material, references to submissions to the post-Higgs consultation are given only to the respondent and the date of the response.

legitimacy in his identity as a company chairman, in addition to his senior non-executive role at HSBC.

Board Design in the 2009–2010, Post-financial Crisis Debate

The issue of overall board structure came up again in the debate leading up to the 2010 code. In the initial consultation in early 2009, with its open invitation to raise matters of interest, several mainstream investors and companies alike chose to emphasise the need for a unitary board.

> We consider that the unitary board model still represents the most appropriate way forward.... We also fully support the continued separation of the roles of chairman and chief executive, and an appropriately balanced board. (ABI, May 2009, p. 2)

> In assessing the merits of these various proposals we have been mindful of the need to ... [p]reserve unitary board structures, with both executive and non-executive directors contributing effectively. (CBI, May 2009, p. 2)

Sentiments like these might appear to be boiler-plate, language dusted off and reused from a previous consultation paper and not of import, except that the issue was still alive among other actors in the field. Some of them were fringe actors, but others, like the Association of Chartered Certified Accountants (ACCA), were closer to the centre. A professional body with longstanding engagement in corporate governance and many of its accountant-members working in corporations, the ACCA would not normally be viewed as peripheral to the field, but its first submission stated:

> As a first step, the FRC should consider the implications of introducing as an option a two-tier board structure and should consider the changes to the Code that would need to be articulated. (ACCA, May 2009, p. 3)

Its argument was that the financial crisis demonstrated that current arrangements had failed. It laid the blame on the failure of non-executive directors to control managers, and on the custodians of the code for permitting an 'untimely' (p. 2) relaxation in 2008 of the constraints on board chairs and audit committee membership. Boards needed greater independence, not less:

> To draw attention to the failure of independent directors is not to say that less reliance should be placed upon them in the future. But consideration needs to be given to addressing the causes of their ineffectiveness.
>
> While two-tier board structures have not always been notably successful, they can contribute to ensuring that the supervisory board directs and oversees, while the management board manages. In practice, much depends on the composition and powers of the two boards in a two-tier structure. (ACCA, May 2009, p. 2)

The early mention in (albeit limited) support for two-tier boards through the debate signals that the idea has legitimacy among at least some actors in the field, even though it remains a largely alien concept.

Contributors on the other side, however, affirm the counterargument but leave it largely unarticulated. The CBI, for example, states that its members, 'including investor members, strongly uphold the UK's unitary board system'; it later states: 'there is also a need to avoid proposals that tend towards two tier boards' (CBI, October 2009). Use of the passive voice here sweeps away any actor, as if the reader—that is, the authors of the code—needed no explanation. The formal terms of the argument were suppressed because its logic was taken for granted (Green, Li, & Nohria, 2009).

Institutionalising Board Design

The unitary board of pre-Cadbury days was the result of mimetic isomorphism, its value often taken for granted. Separation of the roles of chair and CEO, one of the major thrusts of the Cadbury reforms, was in evidence, though far from universal. Post-Cadbury, it became rare, a sign of normative isomorphism, and subsequent enforcement by major investors and their agents meant isomorphism took on a coercive character. Consider the investor outcry when Stuart Rose sought to become executive chairman of Marks & Spencer after having been CEO (Burgess, Rigby, & Braithwaite, 2008). This was an important debate, but there were others. In the next chapter, we consider the debates of the way that codifying corporate governance might affect boardroom ethos and what form compliance with the code should take.

References

Burgess, K., Rigby, E., & Braithwaite, T. (2008, March 10). Investor fury at M&S role for Rose. *FT.com*. Retrieved January 25, 2016, from http://www.ft.com/cms/s/0/1f3cc59e-ee8c-11dc-97ec-0000779fd2ac.html#axzz1PjNs9g5z.

Cousins, J., & Sikka, P. (1993). Accounting for change: Facilitating power and accountability. *Critical Perspectives on Accounting, 4*(1), 53–72. https://doi.org/10.1006/cpac.1993.1003.

Economist. (2011, December 15). Euphemisms: Making murder acceptable. *Economist.com*. Retrieved December 27, 2011, from http://www.economist.com/node/21541767.

Fear, J. (1997). German capitalism. In T. K. McCraw (Ed.), *Creating modern capitalism: How entrepreneurs, companies, and countries triumphed in three industrial revolutions* (pp. 133–182). Cambridge, MA: Harvard University Press.

Green, O. (1992, June 9). Personal view: Why Cadbury leaves a bitter taste, opinion column. *Financial Times*, p. 19. Retrieved from http://global.factiva.com.

Green, S. E., Jr., Li, Y., & Nohria, N. (2009). Suspended in self-spun webs of significance: A rhetorical model of institutionalization and institutionally embedded agency. *Academy of Management Journal, 52*(1), 11–36. https://doi.org/10.5465/amj.2009.36461725.

Greenwood, R., Suddaby, R., & Hinings, C. R. (2002). Theorizing change: The role of professional associations in the transformation of institutionalized fields. *Academy of Management Journal, 45*(1), 58–80. https://doi.org/10.2307/3069285.

Higgs, D. (2003). *Review of the role and effectiveness of non-executive directors*. Retrieved October 15, 2006, from http://www.ecgi.org/codes/documents/higgsreport.pdf.

Kerr, G. (2006). Transformation at BTR. *Journal of the International Academy for Case Studies, 12*(3), 79–101.

Mitchell, A., & Sikka, P. (1993). Accounting for change: The institutions of accountancy. *Critical Perspectives on Accounting, 4*(1), 29–52. https://doi.org/10.1006/cpac.1993.1002.

Montgomery, B. (1989). European Community's draft fifth directive: British resistance and community procedures. *Comparative Labor Law Journal, 10*(3), 429–451.

Nicholson, B. (2008). The role of the regulator. In K. Rushton (Ed.), *The business case for corporate governance* (pp. 100–118). Cambridge: Cambridge University Press.

Roe, M. J. (2003). *Political determinants of corporate governance: Political context, corporate impact*. Oxford: Oxford University Press.

Winter, J. W., Schans Christensen, J., Garrido Garcia, J. M., Hopt, K. J., Rickford, J., Rossi, G., & Simon, J. (2002, January).*Report of the high level group of company law experts on a modern regulatory framework for company law in Europe*. Retrieved June 12, 2020, from https://ssrn.com/abstract=315322.

CHAPTER 7

Ethos and Explanation

Abstract Board design has an impact on the relationship between directors and therefore the ethos of the boardroom. But the code also specifies the nature of compliance, and in the UK establishes a principle that permits explanations of the reasons for non-compliance, which also affects the ethos. This chapter examines in detail how these two issues—the nature of board relationship and what compliance means—and how they remained controversial through repeated revisions.

Keywords Boardroom ethos · Compliance · Explanation

Two other controversies flared up repeatedly during the consultation over the three periods this study examined. One arose because codification meant the creation of an outside source of authority over the interpersonal relationships of directors within the boardroom and the relationships between boards and shareholders. The other—over the nature of compliance—demonstrated how the development of the code established but then also constrained external control over the functioning of boards. Both represented threats to the sovereignty of the board over corporate decision-making.

D. Nordberg, *The Cadbury Code and Recurrent Crisis*,
https://doi.org/10.1007/978-3-030-55222-0_7

Boardroom Ethos[1]

How directors behave—that is, behaviour within boards and between boards and shareholders—has been an important concern of the code since its inception, but one where the codes' authors have accepted that a code could have little direct impact. As a result, the code has sought to deal with behavioural issues by proxy. Structures and procedures seek to limit the discretion of board and, thus, the range of possible behaviour.

Independence of mind aims to encourage constructive boardroom challenge; lacking a mechanism to ensure it, the code settles for definitions of independence in terms of lack of recent business dealings with the company or personal/family ties to executive directors. Some provisions, including controversial ones like board evaluation (Nordberg & Booth, 2019), may prescribe activities of the board in the hope they will lead to changes in behaviour. With the financial crisis of 2007–2009, however, came stronger acknowledgement that these proxy approaches were insufficient.

Board Ethos in the Cadbury Debate

Documents in the Cadbury Archive show the committee's concern the code might miss the target. A hint comes from the chairman's document (CAD-01265) prepared for the committee as it reviewed all the responses to its May 1992 draft report during September, when the committee would agree the thrust and some detail for final report. A note in an appendix called 'Table of Points for Discussion' includes item 12 on 'The Board', where Sir Adrian writes: 'More emphasis on behaviour needed, less on structure?'

That question does not appear in document offered for the committee's deliberations, but several of the changes agreed that day came in response to concerns about excessive prescription and the 'tone' of the draft report, matters that link structure and behaviour. This debate suggests recognition by the committee of the tension between structure and agency in achieving board effectiveness. In his submission to the committee, Richard Lloyd, the Vickers chairman, put it this way:

[1] This section is adapted from an article in the journal *Economics and Business Review* (Nordberg, 2017). It is publicly available under open access and adapted here with permission.

> … your Report perhaps should pay more heed in your final version to certain behavioural aspects which are, in our view, central to a Board's effectiveness.… most U.K. Boards, anyway those of medium-size companies, are probably more intimately involved in the knowledge, understanding and direction of the business than is the case with counterparts across the Atlantic. (CAD-01357)

These 'behavioural aspects' echo the need for the 'presence' and 'use' of knowledge and skills in the Forbes and Milliken (1999) model of board effectiveness. Lloyd links them to the 'genuinely unitary' nature of UK boards, as opposed to the more supervisory approach in the US. Paul Girolami, Glaxo's chairman, worried that the draft cast non-executives as 'watchdogs or guardians' of interests of shareholder or even 'the public':

> We do not see this as the only — or even primary — role of the non-executive directors. They bring to the boardroom independence and outside experience which cannot be provided by the executive directors, and those qualities are (or ought to be) deployed to enhance the general decision-making of the Board on all the aspects of corporate affairs with which it has to deal. The constructive harnessing of this spectrum of experience requires the creation of a team ethos. (CAD-02105)

The equine metaphor of 'constructive harnessing', coupled with the electromagnetic and colourful metaphor in 'spectrum', invokes images the sense of abundant and unruly force channelled to good purpose. Use of 'team ethos' is valorised as a 'creation'.

The self-described 'professional chairman' J. B. H. Jackson put 'a lot of effort into keeping boards united and am nervous of external interventions which could run against this'; he was 'particularly nervous of cultivating the notion that the standards of behaviour anticipated by "the City" differ between executive and non-executive directors' (CAD-02143). Here 'the City'—the financiers in the City of London—is a distant, alien force seeking to divide those 'united' on the board.

Stanley Kalms, chairman of Dixons, wrote about the 'unique cultures' of companies as justifying the assertion that there was 'little benefit in absolute uniformity for its own sake' and warning against a code that 'did not recognise individuality' (CAD-02167). Sir Richard Greenbury, chairman of Marks & Spencer, said companies 'must act as a cohesive unit'; the context makes clear this refers in particular to boards. Moreover, 'whatever Code or Regulation may be in place, the issue [of boardroom power] will be decided by the mix of personalities' (CAD-02343).

These comments emphasise simultaneously the singularity of companies and the unity of boards. They perceive a threat in a one-size-fits-all code; the individuality of personalities within the boardroom contributes to the unity of the unitary board. The purpose this unity-in-individuality served was expressed by the Confederation of British Industry in arguing that the draft

> … understates the contribution which the non-executives can make to the growth of a business: their different experience brings a fresh eye to problems and the development of strategy. (CAD-02349)

Non-executives contribute scarce resources ('experience', 'a fresh eye') for the sake of developing strategy and promoting growth. These views paint a picture in which the board is an exciting place to be, a place where structures enable more than they constrain, a place alive with contradictions and uncertainties, and a place the draft code threatened to disrupt.

Such considerations are largely absent from submissions by investors, their advisors, and accountancy firms. One of the few investors that remarked on it was the insurance company and asset management firm Legal & General. It welcomed the draft's formal definition of differing roles for executives and non-executives but put emphasis not on the *control* function of non-executives but their *service*: 'balance is provided between executive responsibility for day to day management and non-executive strategic input' (CAD-02353). The venture capital and investment company 3i went further, noting that it was worried the draft wanted non-executives to act as 'corporate policeman' when they were needed to contribute to policy development. It installed directors on the companies in which it invested 'to benefit the business not to police our investment' (CAD-02387). It is worth noting that L&G and 3i were themselves major listed companies as well as important investors.

Board Ethos in the Post-Higgs Debate

The Higgs Review of the effectiveness of non-executive directors sought to emphasise the importance of behaviour for the effectiveness of boards. In the body of his report, Higgs added: 'The key to non-executive director effectiveness lies as much in behaviours and relationships as in structures and processes' (2003, Paragraph 6.3), before outlining the 'behaviours and personal attributes' of non-executives (Paragraphs 6.9–6.19). He also provided guidance on the behaviour of effective chairmen in an annex. He used 'behaviour' and 'behaviours' almost interchangeably, leaving readers to interpret to what extent they mean the general depiction of the interaction of directors or observable phenomena. Respondents, particularly but not exclusively from corporations, worried that proposed prescriptions would require specific behaviours, leading to divisions within unitary board and harming performance, rather than fostering trust. We look next at a specific case of their impact: the role of the senior independent director, or SID, and how it would divide the board.

Higgs recommended the SID have a direct relationship with investors. Other non-executive directors meet investors, too, but they should 'rely on the chairman and the senior independent director to ensure a balanced view is taken' (Higgs, 2003, Paragraph 15.16). The SID, by contrast, 'should attend sufficient of the regular meetings of management with a range of major shareholders to develop a balanced understanding of the themes, issues and concerns of shareholders' (2003, Paragraph 15.15). Moreover, Higgs proposed the SID be available to shareholders 'if they have reason for concern that contact through the normal channels of chairman or chief executive has failed to resolve' (2003, Paragraph 7.5).

To many respondents, and especially company chairmen, this challenged the authority of the chairman. The CBI responded in these terms:

> Business is concerned that the proposed Code inadvertently undermines the role of the chairman of a company. It is in no one's interests that this happens. (CBI, 16 April 2003, Paragraph 10)

> We are also very concerned about the proposed role of the senior independent director. Business believes that this could inadvertently create three separate forces in a board whereas boards need to be a united force. The Cadbury Report identified the danger of a CEO dominating the board. What the Report says on the senior independent director actually does increase the potential risk of a CEO playing off the senior independent against the chairman and thereby weakening the chairman. This very much undermines the Cadbury philosophy. (CBI, 16 April 2003, Paragraph 12)

Here the trade association seeks to assert authority by identifying its view with that of 'Business', claiming through a *totum pro parte* authority beyond the scope of its (already powerful) membership. That the 'undermining' is 'inadvertent' seeks to prevent damage without provoking retaliation. By suggesting Higgs might undermine the aims of Cadbury and thus strengthen the hand of the chief executive, the CBI attacks Higgs by invoking the very logic of his review.

Baroness Hogg, chair of the listed private equity group 3i and one of the very few women respondents, said Higgs did 'not sufficiently distinguish between the "backstop" role of the Senior Independent Director, and the day-to-day responsibilities of the Chairman' (2 April 2003). This is the language that defends ('backstop') and thus maintains the status quo and her own role, while seeking to disrupt the changes Higgs planned.

Lord Weir, chair of the construction group Balfour Beatty, argued that the 'promotion' of the SID would 'undermine the role of the Chairman'. His company had not seen the need to follow Cadbury's guidance on designated a senior non-executive in view of the independence of the chairman. Martin Broughton, chair of BAT, said investors 'rarely avail themselves' of the existing opportunity for contact with other directors. Moreover, he called another of the Higgs recommendations—that the chairman not act as chair of the nominations committee or even sit on the audit and remuneration committees—'constitutionally unsound'.

These and other expressions of concern from the corporate side might be seen as chairmen protecting their own positions. But their reasoning invokes corporate benefit arising from trust and collegial behaviour. Moreover, similar sentiments appear in submissions from mainstream investors and their representatives, though in less forceful language. It was a shared issue, if perhaps with different salience to these two core groups.

Board Ethos in the Post-financial Crisis Debate

As the debate got underway in 2009, the Association of British Insurers called attention to relatively new terminology in the field: behavioural governance. The ABI's first submission urged the code-writers to recognise that how people relate is more important than compliance. It did so by drawing a distinction between substance and form:

> In our view the Code, which represents form, can only be effective if the subjects (in most cases the non-executives) apply its principles properly, thereby creating the substance. This application may be termed behavioural governance. Behavioural governance will be affected by such attributes as skills and experience of the individuals, but the two most important attributes a non-executive must have is personal integrity and good judgement. The ABI recognises that it is highly difficult to demonstrate such attributes through a Code, we therefore believe that the most effective way to assess this is through interaction and dialogue between non-executives and investors. (ABI, May 2009, pp. 2–3)

The value descriptors here are 'integrity' and 'judgement' not compliance. The mechanisms are 'interaction' and 'dialogue', though crucially these terms refer to the relationship between directors and investors, placing emphasis on hierarchical accountability rather than mutuality and trust in the boardroom. It acknowledges shareholder primacy while also seeking to move directors' actions away from narrow compliance.

The ABI's submission returned to the theme two pages later when discussing risk management:

> The ability to understand the risks includes an element of judgement. This therefore is an aspect of behavioural governance that investors, as outsiders, will always to a degree struggle to fully grasp. One method of addressing this is to look to 'expert' directors to provide comfort. However, whilst we support the concept of a financial expert on an Audit Committee and relevant expertise being present on the board, we would counsel against over reliance on 'experts'. It is our experience that whilst experts are useful they also have a tendency to be more easily 'captured' as they will naturally see things in a similar manner to other experts, usually management. As important as expert knowledge is, it must be coupled with keen skills of critical analysis, the ability to constructively challenge and question assumptions. Also, other directors may tend to rely too much on the views of the 'expert' rather than bringing their own judgement to bear. (ABI, May 2009, p. 5, punctuation inconsistencies in the original)

The section is worth quoting at length because, unlike other submissions from central actors or its own submissions on other points, the ABI here elaborates its argument, rather than relying upon assumed meanings. Much of the debate preceding the consultation concerned how independent non-executives on bank boards had failed to understand risk. One solution, suggested in the Walker Review two months later, was greater expertise. But here the ABI, a trade association for risk experts, argued *against* expertise, and in rather forceful terms. Experts were 'more easily "captured"', so other directors must bring 'judgement to bear'. The experts themselves must be more than expert; they must also have 'keen skills of critical analysis', and then 'constructively challenge' and 'question assumptions'.

This argument maintains the institution of the code with its emphasis on independence even as it seeks to push it along the path of relying more on behaviour. That the language here is much more vivid than in much of the rest of its submission suggests that its author(s) saw this as a crucial issue. The institutional work is moving in two directions, disrupting the code's reliance on structure and independence while maintaining them as well.

Other submissions also placed emphasis on behaviour more than compliance. The CBI's first submission spoke of the importance of the more general importance of having a 'culture of challenge' in the boardroom, arising from having a 'broad talent pool' of non-executive directors, before adding:

> The effective application of the Code's principles is largely reliant on the behavior [sic] of individuals and their interactions. This is not something that can sensibly be legislated for or regulated. (CBI, May 2009, p. 2)

In contrast to the ABI submission, this account of behaviour and these interactions are internal to the board, not also in relation to shareholders. Moreover, neither the code-writers nor the government can 'sensibly' contribute much to improve it.

The CBI's language affirms the code's value while undermining readings of it that emphasise structure. It denigrates legislation and regulation, implicitly also denigrating the more regulatory approaches to the code implicit in the compliance mentality that other contributors, particularly peripheral actors, had stressed.

The submission from GC100, an association of corporate counsel from the largest companies, made a similar point in suggesting a non-regulatory approach:

> The Code will only provide a framework for good governance but will not alleviate the issues caused by bad management within a company. These behavioural issues can certainly be influenced through a robust

> board/committee evaluation process and possibly through guidance on best practice from the FRC. (GC100, May 2009, p. 4)

This view affirms the value of the code even as it challenges it: the code is 'only' a framework, though the committees it has legitimated can influence behaviour through 'robust' process of evaluation, thus affirming while simultaneously questioning the effectiveness of code. SABMiller identified with the CG100 stance in its submission, before adding:

> If there were governance weaknesses that contributed to the current crisis, it was in the application of the Code rather than a lack of prescription within the Code itself. Adding extra governance requirements is likely to lead to more box ticking and hamper effective scrutiny by non executive directors by occupying time with form rather than looking at substance. Key to the effectiveness of corporate governance is the calibre of the individuals involved, and that they have a clear understanding of their role and responsibilities and the tools necessary to discharge their responsibilities effectively. (SABMiller, May 2009, p. 1)

The contrast between 'form' and 'substance' returns, as do the limitations of codes in dealing with behaviour. Articulation of code creates 'more box-ticking', one of many uses of the derogatory phrase made in submissions from actors in central positions. Emphasis is placed instead on the 'calibre of the individuals' with the 'necessary' tools. That could be read as a request for more tools, had not the passage already warned that extra requirements would 'hamper effective scrutiny' and thus be counterproductive. This is language aimed at maintaining the code, and the logic of corporate governance as SABMiller interprets it, but also to disrupt the plans of others to assert their interpretation of codes as defining acceptable behaviour, not merely providing structures within which agents can act.

As the three consultations progressed, the topic returns from a large number of actors. The CBI's October 2009 submission suggested: 'Promoting a culture of respect, trust and challenge is the most important issue, and ultimately the job of the chairman. The CBI believes that there is only so far you can codify all of this' (p. 3). A few pages later in discussing board evaluation, it added:

> The key aspect of board performance is behavioural, and therefore much less amenable to formal 'testing'. External evaluation should not be a

> substitute for open debate and robust challenge between the Executive and the NEDs, nor effective communication and engagement with shareholders. (CBI, October 2009, p. 6)

Not all respondents agreed. The second submission by Fair Pensions, an advisory firm to pension funds, responded to the FRC assertion that 'There is a recognition that the quality of corporate governance ultimately depends on behaviour not process' in the following terms:

> Everyone accepts that good governance depends on behaviour and that regulation alone is not enough. The practical question, however, is what form of regulation will best promote the required behaviour. (Fair Pensions, October 2009, p. 2)

The word 'however' does the rhetorical change of direction and one that invokes a different, regulatory logic of behaviour more akin to agency than stewardship theory in corporate governance, emphasising more the structure in an institutional approach to the field than the concept of embedded agency. This form of institutional work is both maintaining the code and disrupting attempts of those in more central positions to maintain their understandings of the code.

Voices Present but Missing from This Debate

As an advisory firm on ethical investments, Fair Pensions sits some distance from the centre of the investment field. Theirs were among the few documents from more peripheral actors to make any significant statements about behaviour, and its contribution emphasises the primacy of control through regulation, not cohesiveness, collegiality, and trust. Other non-core actors—whether close intermediates like accountancy firms or lawyers, or more distant ones like academics or proxy voting agencies—also focused on structure and independence, that is, on achieving greater *control*, not the contribution of enhanced *service*. Perhaps they were too removed from what goes on inside the 'black box' of the boardroom (Huse, 2005; Zona & Zattoni, 2007) to feel competent to judge how codes might affect behaviour.

Explain, or Just Comply?

The issue of compliance, which also recurred over the two decades, came in strong language, if not with the same heat as board design. That it was markedly less controversial in the later debates was because it provided the logic that made the code work for all: the principle that complying with the code included non-compliance when accompanied by an explanation, or 'comply or explain'. This elegant fudge appears to have arisen largely spontaneously from within the Cadbury Committee. Through the rest of the consultations over two decades dissenting voices argued that 'comply or explain' left the code with no teeth, or worse: that it had led to a false sense of security that 'good' corporate governance was in place. These were minority views, however, mainly from actors in more peripheral parts of the landscape. In this section we examine the treatment of the concept during the consultations involved in each of the three main versions of the code.

Compliance in the Cadbury Debate, 1992

Records in the Cadbury archive give little hint of the elegant, comply-or-explain solution to the debate they document between proponents of regulation and those who feared heavy-handed regulatory intervention in response to the shocks to the system in the early 1990s.

When the language we now call 'comply or explain' emerged in the draft code in May 1992, it came with aggressive language that implied compliance should be the norm: 'to state whether they are complying with the Code and if not, why not'. That phrase arose in a paragraph about enforcement through the listing regime, which would 'require' as a 'continuing obligation' a statement of compliance. The London Stock Exchange would 'draw public attention' to 'inadequate disclosure'. The final code softened the language to 'or give reasons for non-compliance', which nonetheless left the rhetorical emphasis on compliance. Moreover, the section in which it appeared was headed simply 'Compliance'. The phrase 'comply or explain', which came to symbolise the voluntary nature of the code, did not appear in either the draft or the final document.

Some respondents to the draft, particularly from the corporate side, praised its flexibility, but many argued for more. J. B. H. Jackson, the 'professional chairman', welcomed the link to the listing rules and noted: 'No listed company should be afraid of disclosing non-compliance for good cause' (CAD-02143). But Stanley Kalms, chairman of Dixons whose role at the company in 1992 breached Cadbury's proposed separation of chair and CEO,[2] argued that 'non-compliance ... should not be outlawed' and wanted a 'flexible framework', not a 'straight jacket' (CAD-02167). The language suggests the strength of his feeling. His metaphor associates the implicit alternative—a mandatory code, based in company law—with madness.

Cadbury received support as well from the investor side for a voluntary approach, now explicitly linked to the alternative of a change in law:

> ABI welcomes the emphasis on compliance with a voluntary Code of best practice rather than a statutory Code. The former should encourage greater consistency with the spirit rather than just the letter; the latter is only likely to impose minimum standards. The framework of the Code with accompanying recommendations should enable responsible shareholders to identify deficiencies more readily and take appropriate action at an early stage. (ABI, CAD-02467)

The argument here—that voluntarism will bring compliance with higher standards—echoes the self-disciplinary effects of institutions that come to be accepted through normative rather than coercive isomorphism by relying upon a common cognitive base and a professional network for self-enforcement (DiMaggio & Powell, 1983). Central actors and others like them pushed the committee towards a stance more accommodating of the corporate wish for greater board discretion within the new framework. As such their debates can be seen simultaneously as seeking to repair the proto-institution of the code while undermining the legitimacy of a more extreme interpretation of its meaning.

Compliance in the Combined Code of 2003

By the time of the first major revision of the code, the phrase 'comply or explain' had become embedded in the language of corporate governance around the world. It was used to describe the approach used in countries ranging from South Africa to Sweden. In Germany, the first code

[2] Dixons appointed John Clare as group managing director in 1992 and group chief executive in 1994. Kalms was executive chairman at the time, a title often regarded as involving CEO duality, and was deeply involved in the business he had joined, aged 16, in 1948; he had become chairman in 1971.

of corporate governance incorporated this type of voluntarism despite considerable legal and other structural differences between Germany and the UK. Even in the US, where the legal requirements of Sarbanes-Oxley formed the central response to the Enron collapse, both Nasdaq (2002) and the New York Stock Exchange (NYSE, 2003) used comply or explain to introduce their new listing recommendation separating the roles of chair and CEO.

In the consultation in the UK following the Higgs Review, the mechanism of a voluntary provision was not widely debated; it was evidently not considered a 'fatal flaw' but rather one of the strong points of the corporate governance regime. But respondents worried in unusually vivid language that market developments had morphed its application in ways unanticipated in Cadbury. Viewed from the corporate side, the more prescriptive elements of the Higgs draft code, combined with the enforcement through proxy voting advisers, had led to a risk of 'comply or disdain' (BAT, 5 March 2003) or 'comply or else' (CBI, 16 April 2003). The CBI added in the code it 'should be clearly stated that **to explain is to comply**' [emphasis in the original]. Several respondents used terms similar to those of Sir Brian Moffat, chairman of the steelmaker Corus writing as senior independent director of HSBC. He blamed both the proxy voting firms and the media for the deterioration of meaning in the phrase:

> ... we have real concern with adopting all the Higgs recommendations as a result of experience from the influence of voting recommendations of commercial service providers and the attitude of the U.K. media. Their recommendations and attitude appear to be based on acceptance of 'Comply' but rejection of 'Explain' - a 'box ticking' approach. (Corus, 20 March 2003)

Moffat then stated that the UK 'is fortunate to have a HSBC Holdings plc registered here', citing a 'real risk' that investors outside the UK might misinterpret UK corporate governance. HSBC was previously known as the Hongkong and Shanghai Banking Corporation, and much of its business was in China and East Asia. Moffat's statement was an implicit warning that the bank could move its headquarters abroad if the regulatory regime became too uncomfortable.

In these examples, the iconic language is used to undermine how the code had been used in practice, rather than its letter or spirit. In so doing, these respondents, arguing from the centre of the landscape, reject the way gatekeepers on the periphery had bent the code's symbolic language to purposes other than those of more central actors. Their responses were attempts to return the code to what they saw its original purpose, as voluntary guidance, not a performance metric.

Making this defence of the code simultaneously attacks the extension of it proposed by Higgs to include many more provisions, on the grounds it would lead to even more box-ticking. Lord Weir, chairman of Balfour Beatty, for example, invokes irony to undermine the Higgs recommendations by attacking the enforcers. His letter uses the terms 'the reality is that …' and 'the fact is that …' in the same paragraph, seeking to dismiss the Higgs recommendations as being detached from reality and lacking evidence.

The depiction of the corporate governance staff at investment institutions in that paragraph as 'low-level box-ticking fonctionaires' undermines the legitimacy of investors through a pejorative designation of their roles, suggesting the people, not just the approach they take, are 'low-level'. The structure of the phrase invites a reading of 'box-ticking' as an attribute of individuals, not as a description of an activity they happen to perform. Moreover, selection of 'fonctionaires' mocks both the old enemy (France) and its new replacement (Brussels, that is, the European Union) with just a single word. That sentence goes on, however, to voice its strongest rebuke against investors who do not hire their own 'fonctionaires' but 'even' outsource the process to the 'unadmirable PIRC'. PIRC, the firm called Pension & Investment Research Consultants, was founded in 1986 to advise local authority pension funds on their investments. It was often associated with both shareholder activism and left-wing causes.

This is language that disdains those who measure compliance and ignore explanations. In just four short paragraphs, Lord Weir has used irony to disrupt the attempt to institutionalise practices he sees as counterproductive (the 'unintended consequences' he fears). He seeks to support the code, as he and others like him interpret it, while disrupting the interpretations of other actors from other parts of the corporate governance landscape.

The Dispute Over 'Comply' in the 2009–2010 Debate

In the consultations in 2009–2010, a wider set of voices arose contesting the appropriateness of the 'comply-or-explain' provision. Corporate actors in large numbers urged a change in language to 'apply or explain'. Other respondents, however, remarked that the UK response in 2003 to the crisis of Enron and others had been timid in comparison to changes introduced in the US under the Sarbanes-Oxley Act of 2002 and urged less voluntarism and more compulsion. The CBI's second submission in 2009 addressed both points, while supporting the corporate stance:

> There must be a strong awareness of the need to avoid over-reactions and unintended consequences, and we are mindful of the difficulties that arose in the US as a result of Sarbanes-Oxley. (CBI, October 2009, p. 3)

> The CBI is aware that a number of representations have [been] made that the phrase 'apply or explain' more accurately reflects the spirit of the Combined Code and we would support that view. (CBI, October 2009, p. 8)

GC100, an association of corporate general counsels, and therefore legal professionals with close ties to corporate interests and values, argued the case for 'apply-or-explain' even more forcefully:

> We are concerned that some investors may choose to simply apply the voting recommendations of a proxy agent to their holdings without examining the issues themselves (and indeed we recognise that some investors feel they are not resourced to undertake comprehensive analysis of each company in which they invest during the AGM season, particularly smaller firms). Again, this demonstrates why the Code should encourage 'apply or explain' (rather than comply or explain) as it compels greater engagement and dialogue between companies and their owners on the governance performance of boards. (GC100, October 2009, p. 7)

Moreover, it warned against the FRC or the stock market regulators at the Financial Services Authority becoming directly involved in enforcement:

> This is why 'apply or explain' is a better mantra in this context (and one which Derek Higgs himself had wished he had adopted). (GC100, October 2009, p. 6)

The various submissions lined up on each side of the debate: Several pointed out that the Netherlands corporate governance code had used 'apply', thus invoking a legitimacy inherited from a nearby and closely aligned corporate environment and financial market. Others noted that South Africa, too, had chosen to use the term 'apply', having been one of the first countries to follow the UK down the route of codifying corporate governance and in some submission held up as a paragon that had overtaken the UK as a model of best practice.

The reference in the CG100 submission to Higgs's comments associated its views with a person regarded with considerable reverence by those actors who argued for tighter regulation. By invoking the name of the person who had come to symbolise the other side of the argument, GC100 undercuts the moral position actors who argued that changing this iconic language would signal a significant softening of the code's stance.

Board Ethos, Corporate Explanation

The debate over ethos in these three periods illustrates that what was at stake was the problem at the heart of the work of boards of directors: Is the board a collaborating entity or a forum for challenge? Both approaches carry risks. Collaboration can veer into cosiness and groupthink, challenge into conflict and dysfunctionality. If we see the problem of corporate governance as one of the elites exerting power over corporate resources to the detriment of either shareholders or the general public, we might want the code to promote challenge. If we see the problem instead as sluggish decision-making, poor products, and weak profitability, we might want stronger collaboration. If we see the problem as well-informed executives exploiting information asymmetries for personal gain, we might not want executives on boards at all. Those contributing to the code sought to see their concerns and the values they represent embodied in its text.

If to explain is to comply, then why did we come to say 'comply or explain'? As we have seen the code only adopted that language after the marketplace of ideas had, but then quickly institutionalised it. It became accepted, yes, but never quite taken for granted. The emphasis on 'compliance' in the language of the Cadbury Code arose because there was a problem evident in corporate governance. Boards were not acting ethically, in the sense of having a thoughtful debate over the differing frameworks for deciding what was the right thing to do. Compliance with the mechanisms of the code could build up practices that prevent excesses.

But doing so carries risks. Complying stops thoughtful debate by giving boards a seal of approval that they have done the right thing, even if they haven't.

Let us then revisit what this historical investigation has shown us about the code, the actors who made it, and the voices they heard during the debate. In the next chapter we will look and what those elements tell us about the cycle of ethics, politics, and institutions, as well as discussing voices absent from the recurring debate.

References

DiMaggio, P. J., & Powell, W. W. (1983). The Iron Cage Revisited: Institutional isomorphism and collective rationality in organizational fields. *American Sociological Review, 48*(2), 147–160.

Forbes, D. P., & Milliken, F. J. (1999). Cognition and corporate governance: Understanding boards of directors as strategic decision-making groups. *Academy of Management Review, 24*(3), 489–505. https://doi.org/10.5465/AMR.1999.2202133.

Higgs, D. (2003). *Review of the role and effectiveness of non-executive directors*. Retrieved October 15, 2006, from http://www.ecgi.org/codes/documents/higgsreport.pdf.

Huse, M. (2005). Accountability and creating accountability: A framework for exploring behavioural perspectives of corporate governance. *British Journal of Management, 16*(S1), S65–S79.

Nasdaq. (2002). *Summary of NASDAQ corporate governance proposals*. Retrieved November 3, 2002, from http://www.nasdaq.com/about/Corp_Gov_Summary101002.pdf.

Nordberg, D. (2017). Board ethos and institutional work: Developing a corporate governance identity through developing the UK code. *Economics and Business Review, 3[17]*(1), 73–96. https://doi.org/10.18559/ebr.2017.1.4.

Nordberg, D., & Booth, R. (2019). Evaluating the effectiveness of corporate boards. *Corporate Governance: The International Journal of Business in Society, 19*(2), 372–387. https://doi.org/10.1108/CG-08-2018-0275.

NYSE. (2003). *Final NYSE corporate governance rules*. Retrieved October 15, 2006, from http://www.ecgi.org/codes/documents/finalcorpgovrules.pdf.

Zona, F., & Zattoni, A. (2007). Beyond the black box of demography: Board processes and task effectiveness within Italian firms. *Corporate Governance: An International Review, 15*(5), 852–864. https://doi.org/10.1111/j.1467-8683.2007.00606.x.

business (service)? The issue of ethos goes to the heart of the ethical decision-making of board, their internal processes, and in a sense the sovereignty of directors: Who decides? The issue of compliance concerns the relationship between corporations and the state. Should the code adopt a logic of shareholder primacy and enforcement through market mechanisms? Or should it rely upon state-based institutions (law or regulation), or instead through professional scrutiny (audit)?

Institutions, Logics, and Work in Writing the UK Code

Institutional theorists argue that such logics conflict with each other, but the resolution does not always mean victory for one. Instead, logics may develop into a hybrid form (Ebrahim, Battilana, & Mair, 2014) or become sedimented (Soin & Huber, 2013), with discarded logics buried under successive layers. By contrast, this study shows conscious argumentation over opposing logics, each legitimated through being part in the debate or left open through ambiguity. While there is evidence of logic-blending in the code's division of unitary boards into executive and non-executives, with different functions, defeated logics are not so much sedimented, buried under layers, but instead present and yet not enacted, in a word, suspended.

An Institution in Search of a Logic

Throughout these consultations, actors sought to win their arguments and appeals to logics that had been legitimated in other organisational fields. Even when they made assertions, rather than arguments, the voices in the debate spoke as though their logics were understood and thus taken for granted, as institutional theory suggests. Moreover, some attempted to import competing logics from Europe or the US to the UK. That the arguments these logics entail often remained suppressed suggests that other actors already accept, at one level or another, the legitimacy of these solutions.

For example, in 1992 Charkham (CAD-01073) called for 'real accountability' without definition, inviting Sir Adrian Cadbury to import his own meaning. In 2003, the language used by company chairs in urging changes in the text invited the FRC to interpret their calls either as signs of their stewardship and a logic of superior managerial knowledge, or as a signal of the legitimacy of shareholder value maximisation based on markets. In 2009–2010, the ACCA's call for German-style boards with worker co-determination rests explicitly on a logic embracing shareholder value maximisation. But it imports with it an implicit and unstated acceptance of the legitimacy of co-determination and with it a logic based on the value of a wider community. That the latter is unstated leaves other actors in the field free to translate the call to suit their understanding and see in it heightened monitoring and control.

Over the course of the three periods, many of those supporting unitary boards came from the central actors. Companies and their collective associations (particularly the CBI) made strongly worded statements but rarely reasoned arguments. Their central position did not need a defence; rather, the code—a voluntary, not statutory institution—required their assent. Theirs was an assertion that current arrangements were not just appropriate, but superior to the alien concepts of European, German, or indeed American practice.

Mainstream institutional investors supported this view; some such actors were themselves listed companies and sat on both sides of the corporate/investor divide. The advantages of incumbent institutional arrangements were taken for granted, so much so they scarcely needed argumentation. Investors in general did not make their cases based on what agency theory would lead us to think was their interest, in enhancing monitoring and control through board structure. Their logic might reasonably arise from a market orientation, with its focus on the transaction, shareholder primacy and narrow self-interest.

It might seem reasonable to assume that listed insurance companies would face contradictory logics. What we see, however, is something rather different: an absence of conflict, even from investors that were not listed companies or from individuals not in positions representative of corporate imperatives. Theirs was in the main a hybrid logic, claiming shareholder primacy but accepting the risk of managerialism in that non-executive directors might be captured by the executives for the sake of performance through collegiality and the 'service' function of directors.

Accountancy firms echoed the sentiments of corporations and investors on this point, though not universally and not with assumption that the incumbent position needed no defence. But the profession was undergoing its own institutional change during this time involving a contest between professional and commercial logics (Hinings, Brown, & Greenwood, 1991; Suddaby & Greenwood, 2005). During this period accounting firms began to act more like corporations, selling management, information technology, and human resources consultancy services to corporate clients. By the early 2000s, such services would dwarf audit as the source of revenue, putting professionalism on the back foot.

Let's recall that by 2003, the venerable audit firm Arthur Andersen had ceased to exist. Its implosion arose as advisory work for Enron, WorldCom, and others proposed and then validated financial arrangements that led ultimately to their bankruptcies. Perhaps these actors were more sensitive to corporate interests and values than those of investors.

Those supporting two-tier boards and therefore institutional change came, with important exceptions, from more peripheral positions in the field. Their arguments draw upon a language of high performance, secure investments, and long-term orientation, characteristics of German corporate performance. These are sentiments associated more with collectivism and ideas of shared commitment.

Actors straddling the debate were an eclectic bunch, in part peripheral, in part more central to the field. Some suggested novel approaches (e.g. the Liberal Democrats in 1992); others endorsed experimentation (Arthur Andersen in 1992 and, it seems, Sir Adrian Cadbury himself). They were what DiMaggio (1988) calls institutional entrepreneurs, agitating for change of less specific character to address evident failings in current institutional arrangements. Their arguments embody assumptions or show the willingness to cross boundaries.

How this debate was resolved has had a variety of effects on the relationship between corporations and investors and on the relationships among other actors across the field. It shaped the language of corporate governance, gained acceptance, and built a community.

The question of compliance adds another layer: The debates we have seen involved the threat of state action, but the context meant that solutions in law and regulation seemed out of reach. The consultation for the Cadbury Code, echoed in later revisions, paid only limited attention to another possibility: that enforcement, and with it an assertion of (non-)compliance, might have fallen to the audit profession, rather than investors. Submissions from the accountancy firms and professional bodies made no strong pitch for the business. If anything, the absence of such suggests that these matters lie outside their will and perhaps their competence.

Neither the Cadbury debate nor subsequent consultations provide the evidence, but it seems possible that Sir Adrian's own roots in the corporate world and boards may have left the question of auditing corporate governance unasked. One reason for empanelling the Cadbury Committee was the perceived failure of the profession to spot the problems with the financial aspects of corporate governance. Asking auditors to oversee compliance might well have been unthinkable in 1991–1992; assigning the role to investors had become institutionalised when later versions were underway and were perhaps not open for discussion. However, the audit profession's reputation had, if anything, deteriorated further, after Enron and again after the financial crisis.

Institutional Work in Corporate Governance[1]

Writing the code was in general a conservative process throughout the period. Despite crises of legitimacy, these efforts arose largely outside political and legislative purview. As a consequence, the actors engaged in them were largely those with vested interests in incumbent practices as much as future outcomes. Those conditions suggest processes where little institutional change would emerge and the work done would be mainly of the 'maintaining' varieties in Lawrence and Suddaby (2006).

Work in 1992. Cadbury's work was institutional entrepreneurship (DiMaggio, 1988), seizing an opportunity when legitimacy of established practices had come into question. The process, including the consultations and the informal meetings, research, and media coverage that surrounded it, provided repeated opportunities for the work that Lawrence and Suddaby (2006) call educating, theorising, defining, and vesting. The consultation worked by constructing normative networks among contributors and between them and the drafting committees and individuals. The initial work changed normative associations by connecting intended practices with moral underpinnings, which were reinforced by the association of the Cadbury family over generations with practices we now call social responsibility. Cadbury was the moral face of capitalism; Maxwell was the opposite.

Enlisting important industrialists for the committee and soliciting views from others brought potential opponents into a position where they needed to articulate their position from within the frame Cadbury's draft had set. In contributing to the debate, opponents construct identities

[1] This sub-section and the next are adapted from the article Nordberg (2017) and used with permission.

not too far removed from terms the draft had given; its new mechanisms then facilitate diffusion of the new practices, or at least their translation (Czarniawska & Joerges, 1996) by actors less than thoroughly convinced by the arguments they have heard. This echoes the projective agency in the version of institutional work in Battilana and D'Aunno (2009). But holding open competing views through the comply or explain regime, the code that emerged allows actors in the field to keep multiple identities following different logics in a kind of suspended animation as they incorporate the code in their own practice. This identity work (Creed, Dejordy, & Lok, 2010; Lok, 2010) suggests a need to add another type of practical-evaluation agency to Battilana and D'Aunno's phase of creating institutions.

Work in later versions. Subsequent major versions paint a more complex picture. With a formal code in place, the canvas that Higgs and then the FRC used in 2003 was not blank. Existing practices from Cadbury had been institutionalised over a decade and mythologised, a form of 'maintaining' work (Lawrence & Suddaby, 2006). Through the iconic status of the code around the world, those practices had won over critics from 1992. Contributions to the 'fatal flaws only' review in 2003 suggest that many had come to identify with Cadbury precepts, including ones they had viewed as radical in 1992. That is, these organisations, and in some cases individuals, had learned to adapt through translation and bricolage to use the code and still suit their companies' circumstances.

They praised the Higgs Review (2003) and its insights into non-executive directors, a form of 'valorising', but disputed its recommendations, 'demonising' as alien in their attempt to split the board. This is work by these actors that Lawrence and Suddaby would call 'maintaining' incumbent arrangements, but it also disrupts the entrepreneurship in Higgs. Nicholson faced that fury with a fudge. He converted Higgs's recommendation of a definition of independence involving a six-year tenure into what came to be called the 'nine-year rule' created in the 2003 Combined Code. That was work that Battilana and D'Aunno (2009) would call 'repairing' or a change Lawrence and Suddaby (2006) would see as 'enabling'—both of the 'maintaining' variety—but maintaining *entrepreneurial* ideas, while disrupting existing arrangements.

In 2010, Sir Christopher Hogg's changes to the code recognised issues left untreated in the Cadbury and Higgs inquiries, that the boardroom ethos was more important than structures or formal definitions of independence. Contributions to that consultation nonetheless brought up old ideas and issues up for reconsideration, ideas that sought again to address questions of structure and definitions of independence. The institutional work was a repeat of prior attempts by some to repair and others to undermine the moral associations of a code that had failed to prevent a recurrent wave of governance failings. What emerged, however, was advocacy of translation and bricolage, and advocacy of de-institutionalisation through explanations rather than compliance. The 2010 code picked up and amplified a subtext of the discourse that spoke of the limitations of code and the need for a combination of trust and challenge, respect within critique, that corporate actors and some others had advocated since the earliest days, but which previous authors of the code had reflected only in part. Was this work disrupting existing arrangements, maintaining the spirit by repairing the language, or creating something rather different?

Actors from different parts of the broader field of corporate governance would view these examples of work differently. Those that start with a logic of control as the purpose of boards could find the advocacy from corporations and the actions of the author in the 2010 process as disrupting to the central purpose corporate governance. Those that start from a logic of service, of the board as a solution to resource constraints, could see in the 2010 process invention and advocacy of a new set of arrangements that simultaneously undermined incumbent ones.

Work as contingent on position in field. This discussion suggests the concept of institutional work is contingent on the position of the actors in the broader field: work one actor might view as maintaining an institution is one that disrupts diffusion of arrangements that others advocate, a somewhat different view from that developed by Creed and colleagues (2010). In their case, marginal actors committed to the institutions acted as change agents, thus simultaneously maintaining and disrupting it. Here, actors hold differing interpretations of the key tenets of institution—what constitutes board effectiveness—and its logic—control or service—each supported by texts and discourses that permit adherents to hold them in contradiction. This is true particularly for this case, because the field is unsettled.

Codification and Identity

This study demonstrates processes of institutional work creating the code and then helping it to evolve it over time. The initial hostility to provisions in Cadbury seen as disrupting the ethos of UK boards was diminished and in some cases no longer present later on. That is, the institutionalisation of the code has taken hold as individuals and organisational actors adapted their practices and found ways to sustain the elements of ethos of boards. When the subsequent revision after the Higgs Review challenged their understandings of board ethos, those voices argued for Cadbury but against its extension into a more confrontational board, but then lost the argument. By 2010, however, the process of codification reopens the debate about ethos and, without rolling back the provisions installed through Higgs, urges greater use of explanation rather than compliance, acknowledging the fears that corporate governance had become oppressive to the way boards work.

Through the process of codification—that is through the institutional work of creating, maintaining, and occasionally seeking to disrupt the code—contributors' views moderate. Actors from the investment side voice ideas identified with corporate economic interests. Similarly, corporate actors come to voice sentiments that acknowledge investor interests. Some non-core actors' views also converge, as they identify through the processes of codification and institutional work with an emerging logic of corporate governance itself. This reflects what individuals active in the UK corporate governance field have remarked anecdotally that individuals identify as corporate governance specialists, sometimes more strongly than with the organisation and field (corporations, investor, advisor, agitator) in which they work.

Process of Codification

This study also suggests that the process of repeated consultation and drafting contributes to the successful development and diffusion of codes of conduct. In these examples, codification arose through a process with the following stages: An existing set of practices, widely if not universally accepted, is unsettled by a shock to the system widely seen as internal to the system if perhaps external to many actors within it. That jolt places the equilibrium of current arrangements in question. Through services of a (more or less) trusted intermediary, views from both the centre and the most distant parts of the field are aired and definitions of accepted terms questioned. In those circumstances, authorship matters. Through one or more iterations, the author decides the terms in which the debate takes place, that is, the language in use. That language creates the discourse that legitimates certain categories of actors, activities, and forms of organising, ready for codification. Enactment of those forms and activities by multiple actors across the field alters social practice, legitimating the discourse, and reinforcing the texts (Fairclough, 1992).

This study suggests that central to the success of codification are three factors: (a) the opening of the terms of the debate, (b) the services of a trusted mediator/author, and (c) the sense of broadly shared values among participants, which prevent the debate becoming reduced to narrowly self-interested negotiations. In so doing, they avoid the interest dissatisfaction and clash of value commitments Greenwood and Hinings (1996) see as prior conditions for institutional change. Further research could help to establish this. The process is summarised in the map seen in Fig. 8.1.

Central to the success in this example of codification, which involves powerful elites agreeing to cede discretion, seem to be two further factors this study has analysed only tangentially: (d) the promise of an iterative cycle, with or without a fresh jolt to the system; and (e) the 'escape clause' of comply or explain, which permits differentiation with a unified response. The iterations of the single loop of learning in this diagram hold out the promise of more satisfactory outcomes in the future, but it impedes development of the double-loop reflexivity associated with more radical changes in incumbent arrangements (Veldman & Willmott, 2016).

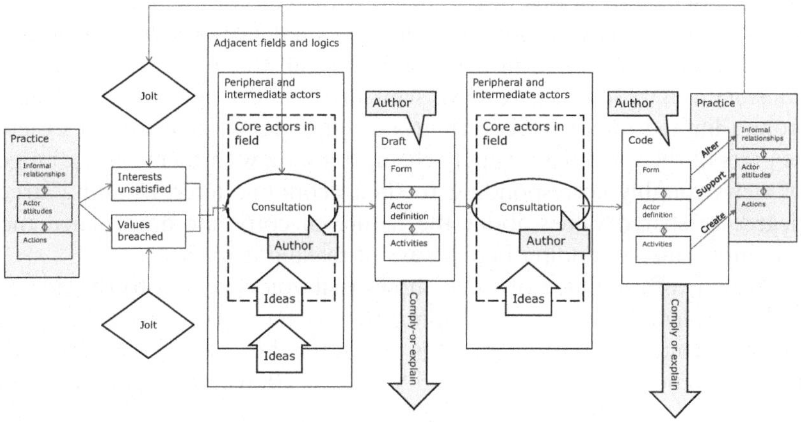

Fig. 8.1 Codification process

In the case of the UK codes of corporate governance, the jolts leading to the versions of 1992 and 2010 were in many ways home-grown and of considerable magnitude, increasing their force and injecting urgency into the need for change and thus the salience of the calls from change from more peripheral voices. Ideas from what we might call adjacent organisational fields—from the German model of corporate governance or the European Union's deliberations—get a hearing.

The version of 2003 is somewhat different, in that the jolt was clearly from outside. The problems at Enron, WorldCom, and others in the US were based in a governance system that made little use of executive directors and much use of rules-based regulation of corporate affairs and accountancy. Contributions to the Cadbury inquiry suggest UK directors saw these not just as less effective but also as alien.

Even the problems that affected European companies at the time came from alien systems: Ahold had a two-tier board; Parmalat had a governance system seemingly modelled on the Maxwell empire of pre-Cadbury days. Those corporate actors rejected the specific Higgs provisions, sometimes in quite forceful language, suggests insufficient interest dissatisfaction or conflict of values to evoke change (Greenwood & Hinings, 1996). But changes happened nonetheless, suggesting the shared values about the greater purpose of corporate governance overcame the inertia of an institutionalised field.

The discussions of board design and compliance, as well as the debate over boardroom ethos, show roots in the experience of individual actors, and not just corporate entities responding abstractly to the issues the consultations raised. As we have seen in these examples of the debate from a limited sample of contributors, respondents came from a variety of parts of the investment supply chain, bringing with them both a range of views roughly corresponding to their economic interests and a large degree of shared values about the nature of corporate governance and the importance of finding better ways of making it work.

Analysis of the range of views shows that voices central to the debate had considerable impact on shaping the content of the codes, at least in part through advocating changes practice and in code, in keeping with the expectations of Greenwood and Suddaby (2006). Their positions held greater salience (Mitchell, Agle, & Wood, 1997) with the codes' authors, in that they more urgent in terms of the impact on their activities, more legitimate if judged from the perspective of invested funds and effort, and certainly more powerful. As Sir Adrian Cadbury's notes show in several places, had the code authors not won commitment from associations like the ABI and CBI, from key institutional investors and from the chairs of influential companies, their efforts might have been stillborn, despite strong 'precipitating jolts' (Greenwood, Suddaby, & Hinings, 2002) in the field.

On occasion, single voices, like those of Sir Owen Green during the Cadbury inquiry, provided a rallying point for others, crystallising their own thinking in language that exercises force over those tasked with writing the code and changing the terms of the debate and possibly its direction. Voices from the periphery of the field, however, contributed ideas that forced reconsideration of positions by those in the centre, in keeping with the expectations of Rao and Giorgi (2006). Those in intermediate positions in the investment supply chain, like the large accountancy firms and other advisers, may have less urgency and power, but their expertise dealing with boards gives them salience, even when their legitimacy, post-Enron, comes into question. Their position allows them to bring new and occasionally challenging ideas into the debate, with authority arising from their independence, even when that independence is based on professionalism brought into question by their own actions.

The shared values of the participants are perhaps the greater surprise of this study. Across the spectrum of opinion, what is evident in the Cadbury inquiry is acknowledgement of the need for change towards more formalised and normative institutional arrangements to supplement or replace the informal ways that boards operated and distilled each other's ideas of best practice. In the post-Higgs and post-financial crisis debates we see acceptance among actors of the need for renewing legitimacy if not about the changes needed to achieve that. Nonetheless, that institutional investors and corporate chairs frequently spoke in the same terms suggests that more than narrow self-interest is at work. The contributions of even the more distant actors show adherence to many of the same principles, such as the need to balance the control functions of the board against its service roles, and perhaps the sense that those two functions cannot easily be distinguished from each other.

Only the most distant of actors lacked a common language of governance with those in the centre; others shared the same terms, if sometimes only through ambiguous definitions. Most adhered to logics that—even when competing for attention during the process of writing the code—contained overlapping meanings for the participants. That the values were shared, if unevenly and with variation, has implications for the process of codification and the nature of the institutional work involved in their authorship.

Experimentation, and the Lack Thereof

What was missing from these debates was the willingness to embrace the spirit reflected in Sir Adrian Cadbury's handwritten notation of the Arthur Andersen submission. Before the 1994 review of the code—which decided to make no changes—Cadbury sought advice about whether anything in law prevented companies from adopting two-tier boards. Having received assurances it did not, no further action took place. As we have seen, the issue of two-tier boards did not go away, but when it returned it was an alternative imperative, a replacement to the unitary board, with the challenge to deeply embedded, institutionalised practices, and the opposition solidified. Two-tier boards were an alien invention, not home-grown. They were associated with the European Community and later the European Union, pressure from the 'fonctionnaires' in Brussels. And in the German-style version, with worker co-determination, it was an assault too close to the spirit of the old Labour Party from the time of the Cadbury debate.

Had the code encouraged experimentation, taking away any imperative or even a hint of preference, what might have happened? Supervisory boards were not entirely alien to the UK landscape, even before Cadbury. British charities had boards that worked *de jure* as supervisory entities. Charity executives reported and still report to an entirely voluntary board; these executives have no voting power of charity policy. That's only a short toss of a stone away from the two-tier board of the Dutch or Swiss variety.

Experimentation with board structures might have been tried in conjunction with external, perhaps even academic research to determine where the advantages and pitfalls lie. Opposition to separate supervisory and management boards is not just a prejudice against things European or labour-friendly. The separation has known drawbacks in terms of strategy formation and restricted information flows (Bezemer, Peij, de Kruijs, & Maassen, 2014; Maassen & van den Bosch, 1999).

Such experimentation might also have been tried in the configuration of board committees. There were precedents, albeit in other countries. Swedish companies have shareholder representatives on committees to nominate new directors (Dent, 2012; Nachemson-Ekwall & Mayer, 2018). In Nigeria, a country whose legal system bears much similarity to Britain, audit committees of listed companies should have equal numbers of shareholder representatives and directors (CAMA, 1990). Such mechanisms have drawbacks, of course, in that the shareholders represented are often the largest holders; their representatives and might represent one shareholder's interest rather than reflecting shareholders' interests more generally. But experimentation without compulsion might have yielded fresh insights. In short, experimentation might have pointed towards possible board figurations that defied both dominant models and represented clear innovation.

Institutionalising such experimentation might have permitted different board cultures to develop and with them an ethos of independence of mind. That might have impeded efforts by investors to look for simple ways to monitor performance through governance ratings that measure corporations' own declarations of director independence based on recent histories related party transactions or kinship. Those are poor proxies for factors like 'independence of mind' and 'boardroom challenge' and thus prevented the box-ticking much despised by corporate actors.

As for compliance, the rhetorical shift from 'comply-or-explain' to 'apply-or-explain' would have cleared up a linguistic lapse. As several respondents in each of the phases noted, to explain is to comply, so the 'or' in the famous phrase makes no sense. Let's recall too that the Cadbury Code and Report did not use that expression, and indeed softened its language between the May 1992 draft and the December 1992 final report. This signal got lost in the noise about compliance, and the rhetoric, once embedded and institutionalised, proved hard to shift. Moreover, as 'comply' was retained in later version, the 'losers' in the battle over two-tier boards could at least claim a small victory for greater public accountability of boards and management.

Here, too, however, encouraging experimentation, rather than just accepting 'explanation', might have yielded more innovative practices. It might have avoided entrenching divisions among what was otherwise coming together with a new community of—a new collective identity as—corporate governance people, which seemed to develop among those individuals who engaged with the processes of the consultation. Experimentation and learning from experience are hallmarks of a pragmatic view that seems to have underpinned the development of the code in these three time periods, but less so its implementation. They acknowledge the uncertainties in the decision made in complex situations and the historical contingency of the rules this new institution would set.

Revisiting the Framework of Corporate Governance

Recalling the ethics-politics-institution framework outlined in Chapter 2, the problem that confronted the Cadbury Committee was new and ethical, even if the corporate malfeasance and misbehaviour that necessitated the effort was not. The committee and Sir Adrian himself had to search their consciences as well as the opinions of the affected publics to find a solution. The process they invented set those ideas out for contestation, informally at first, with little value judgement beyond the need to do something. After the May 1992 initial draft, the process became political. The draft text galvanised respondents to use more forceful language to defend their interests, yes, but also to defend what they valued in the existing and largely informal arrangements.

What emerged from that political phase was the code, a proto-institution on the way to institutionalisation as the process itself, and the person of its author, conveyed legitimacy to the recommended course of action. The ethical debate concerned the ethos of corporate governance. The political contestation was a fight over who holds the power over corporate resources. The institution that emerged—the code with its promise of renewal and review—created a set of rules—principles and recommendations—that make ethical decisions about further rule-making redundant. Let's look at each phase in turn.

Ethics and Ethos

The consultations worked through more than just the exchange of documents used in this study. In each time period, many seminars and workshops occurred, where the topics at issue came together. I took part in a half dozen such events during the 2003 code revision and again during 2009–2010. At these debates, as well as in the submissions to the consultations, participants from across the investment supply chain worried that taking too rigid an approach, steps that might put non-executive directors at loggerheads with the executives, would erode the ethos, the collective sense of collective responsibility, and reduce the desire of outsiders to serve on corporate boards. The fun of helping to shape strategy, of creating value rather than just compliance, seems to be one of the strong motivations about corporate non-executives. The drawbacks of two-tier boards seem to reside with the enhancement of their 'control' function at the expense of 'service'. Proponents of two-tier boards seem to urge directors to become the corporate governance police, apprehending errant executives and deterring their worst tendencies.

The trick in corporate governance seems to be creating the balance of knowledge and skills, behaviour, persuasion, and challenge, and to find individuals who embody all of them, all the time. Superstar directors of this description are surely, logically, very rare indeed. So again, the code may have missed opportunities to encourage playfulness in the shape and composition of boards, and the emotional and cultural intelligence in the boardroom by focusing on approaches that could be verified by scales and valances accessible to the outside world.

In a different context—one related to delivering public services, rather than private profit—the Cambridge philosopher Onora O'Neill has urged people at the top of organisations to engage in what she called 'real' and 'intelligent' accountability, which arises in face-to-face exchanges, repeated over time, in which trust can develop alongside challenge (O'Neill, 2002). She contrasted it with the managerialism in public services that started during Margaret Thatcher's time in power, as government departments sought to develop a culture of performance monitoring based on the experience in private enterprise, which came to be known as the New Public Management (Hood, 1995). This NPM approach relied on using metrics that could be verified externally, giving public accountability for public funds. O'Neill worried that managerialism would detract from the deep, interpersonal form of accountability that draws out individuals' conscience and thoughtfulness, the thoughtfulness of ethical decision-making (see Fig. 8.2).

Politics and Power

The debate about the code took the ethics of authors and the ethos of the board into the pit of politics and power. Much of the institutional entrepreneurship that might have contributed to greater experimentation arose on the periphery of the field of corporate governance, from actors who were unlikely to take power (e.g. Liberal Democrats) or expressed concern about and marketed themselves as supported themes in investments like social responsibility and environmentalism. They lacked

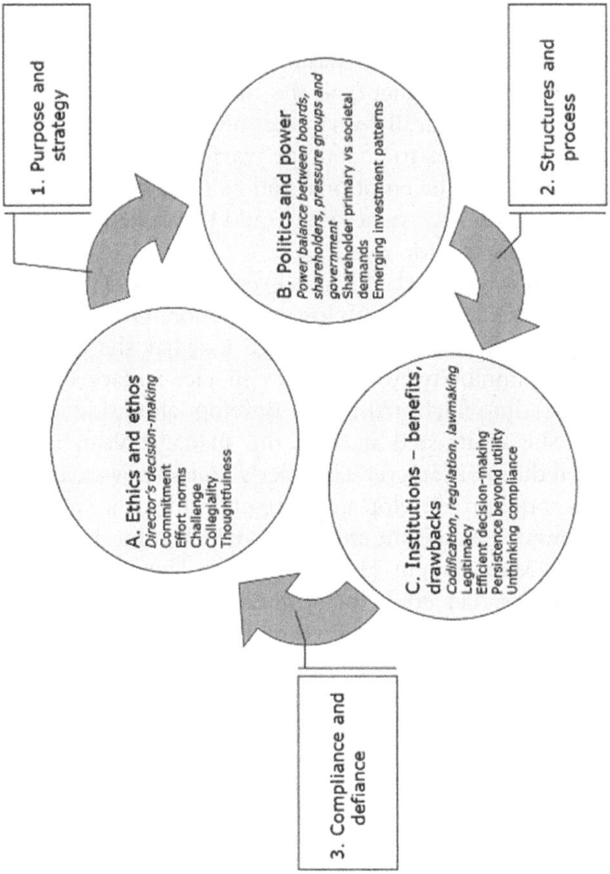

Fig. 8.2 Framework of board decisions, revisited

the political support to influence public policy directly and the financial weight to affect market forces to support their directions.

However, participation in the consultation provided a platform for their views; their rhetoric achieved some level of valorisation and with it, legitimacy. The legitimacy afforded those ideas a place in the evolving discourse of corporate governance. It seems reasonable to assume, and further research could substantiate, that the echoes of the public debate over the code echoed in the media. It certainly did in the *Financial Times*, Sir Owen Green's vehicle of choice to oppose Cadbury. The newspaper was and continues to be an important venue for such debates (see Lok, 2010). The shift of tone in the middle of the field—the consultants and especially the accountancy profession—reinforced the legitimacy that peripheral actors sought. The strengthening of this rhetoric has a constraining influence on the power of more central actors.

At the centre of these debates stood two categories of actors: corporations and institutional investors. There is some overlap between them; listed insurance companies and asset management firms that are themselves listed companies sit in both camps. But their interests conflict: The story of corporate governance, from the 1970s with its theorising of the agency problem (Fama & Jensen, 1983; Jensen & Meckling, 1976), through the Cadbury Code to the present, is one that pits a logic of managerialism against a logic of shareholder value (Lok, 2010; Westphal & Graebner, 2010).

In the Cadbury debate, the structures associated with both board design and the locus of compliance and enforcement shifted power to investors and reinforced their primacy during major revisions. The Higgs-inspired 2003 code, with its focus on board independence stopped short of introducing two-tier boards by the back door. But the power of independent, non-executive directors was a victory for investors, and the code retained its provisions that accountability was upwards, to investors. Nordberg and McNulty (2013) describe how the code, through its revisions, articulates a logic of accountability, and with the 2010 revision that accountability becomes more relational—relations within the board and between the board and investors. The latter is based, however, on its language endorsed investor stewardship, the practicality of which scholars and practitioners alike viewed with scepticism (Cheffins, 2010; Roach, 2011; Wong, 2010). The processes needed for investor stewardship seem to include the formation of a sense of psychological ownership, that is an emotional as well as cognitive commitment to object of that stewardship.

Institutional investors rely however, on processes that involve erecting obstacles to this kind of commitment, discouraging such active engagement, as McNulty and Nordberg (2016) detail. Investor activism seems more in evidence now than stewardship (Filatotchev & Dotsenko, 2015). With it has come a contest for control over corporate policy.

In short, the processes of the writing of the Cadbury Code were marked by mainstream investors asserting a moral high ground based on claims of shareholder primacy and residual rights. Corporations, represented by company chairs, general counsels and non-executives with networks developed in their own corporate experience, defended their territory with claims of the superiority of unitary boards, with their focus on the service role of directors, even as their control side is strengthened through the structures the code imposes. The mainstream investors' claims to primacy, for the separation of powers in the boardroom, and over investor voice were the most influential in writing and then re-writing the code. Whether these actors continue to have the legitimacy depends in part on the inertia of an institutionalised logic as it confronts a changing market context.

Institutionalisation—Benefits and Drawbacks

The code has become an institution in corporate governance, something between the formal and informal institutions in the formulation of Douglass North (1990). It achieved legitimacy, in part through the credibility and personal integrity of its initial main author, Sir Adrian Cadbury, and sustained it through a succession of well-regarded practitioners (Greenbury, Hampel, Turnbull, Higgs) lending both their names and their efforts to seek out ideas. Its durability in the face of the pressure that came from repeated corporate governance crises no doubt arises from the degree of acceptance that the process of its drafting and redrafting has generated. And yet …

The lack of experimentation and innovation, the uniformity of compliance and the self-satisfaction we can detect in the corporate governance sections of company annual reports could also be seen as a sign of complacency, as well as compliance. Let's remember that Royal Bank of Scotland had complied with all but one, very minor provision of the code at the time of its spectacular collapse in September 2008. Yes, the business problem that provoked its demise could be traced directly back to the US government's decision not to bail out the investment bank Lehman

Brothers, just days before. But the decisions of RBS—to invest heavily in US capital markets, to pursue global investment banking, to swell its balance sheet to the largest of any bank in the world, and then to engage in a contested takeover bid for the Dutch bank ABN-Amro—were made by a (unitary) board of directors, with a clear majority of non-executive directors, and a chair who met all the formal criteria of independence from management. Compliance with the code was no defence against collapse.

Institutionalisation brings legitimacy, which can then outstay its welcome. Institutions persist because they create stability and thus can become unresponsive to changes in the competitive, political, and economic environment (Meyer & Rowan, 1977). In the case of the UK code, and despite the flexibility afforded by 'comply-or-explain', codification gave a series of targets that could be monitored at a distance. Investors outsourced the tracking of compliance to information providers and then acted as if the 'rules of the game' in the code were laws of nature. We can see this in the corporate complaints of box-ticking through this study. The implication is that institutional investors—the designator enforcement arm of the Cadbury system—stopped thinking about what compliance meant, creating the condition of 'comply-or-else'. Little wonder, then, that corporate boards stopped thinking about innovative solutions to the governance problem they faced.

Rather than forcing compliance, the code permitted—and the 2010 code encouraged—the use of explanations. This built-in freedom from the code permitted the 'defiance' sketched in the model in Chapter 2 could prevent de-institutionalisation when the rules—the principles and recommendations of the code—did not fit the circumstances of the company, its business, and its market and institutional context. This should have allowed and even encouraged thoughtful, ethical boards to choose a different road from the ones endorsed by the code (see Fig. 8.2).

This favourable outcome depends on boards being thoughtful and ethical, however. The benefit of the code—and its institutionalisation—comes from creating a regime that works even if boards are not particularly thoughtful. It provides a mode of decision-making—at least about structure and independence that prescribes paths that are 'reasonable' and 'good enough' (Nordberg, 2018, 2020). What institutionalising a code cannot protect against, but might discourage, is that a board will be thoughtful but also *un*ethical, a board that hides behind the code and games the system.

As it turned out, corporate boards complied, lest they face the wrath of institutional investors, and sometimes, for good reasons, found ways to comply with the letter of the code while circumventing it in practice. Institutional investors—particularly the mainstream investors from the pension, insurance, and collective investment sectors—became even more deeply embedded in the structures that the code had created than they had before. That entrenched their power, made them, like the corporations in which they invested, defensive about alternative approaches. Change is disrupting.

But change keeps coming, and the context of UK investment—like equity investment around the world—has been changing all the time, and in ways that raise question about the continuing legitimacy of the process of codifying corporate governance.

Fit with the Changing Context—Can the Centre Hold?

The voices heard in the debates in 1991–1992, 2003, and 2009–2010 were remarkably similar and in some cases identical. Large UK corporations, which were household names or mainstays of market index, took part in the debates. Peripheral voices advocating stakeholder rights or responsibilities to other constituencies were largely ignored. Traditional institutional investors—the insurers, pension funds, unit trusts, and investments trusts —have either directly or through their trade associations had a large impact on shaping the code through their engagement in the consultation processes described above. Their contributions legitimated the Cadbury Code, through the broad social and legal acceptance of a principle of shareholder rights and perhaps even shareholder primacy and gave a strong steer in subsequent versions.

But over that period, there have been, and are today, changes afoot in the investment landscape in Britain and around the world. They affect the constellation of actors among the investors themselves, among other actors in the investment supply chain, and among the corporations to which the code applies. These factors all have implications for the future legitimacy of the process of codification.

Changing Investors

The deep engagement of mainstream investors in the process clearly lent legitimacy to the code over the period we have reviewed. However, those traditional, domestic institutions now hold directly less than 20% of the value of UK equities. Missing almost entirely from the later debates were the new actors in the field, notably sovereign wealth funds, hedge funds and the large investors from the United States and other countries; by 2012 they held the majority of UK shares (see Fig. 8.3) and according to data from the Office of National Statistics, their influence has continued to grow (ONS, 2020).[2] Their influence on corporate decision-making is considerable, as shareholder activism has gained force from the affirmation of the special position of institutional investors as guardians of the corporate governance in Cadbury and since.

The financial crisis gave new impetus to shareholder activism in many countries (Becht, Franks, Grant, & Wagner, 2015; Goranova & Ryan, 2014; McNulty & Nordberg, 2016), which may have the consequence of focusing the attention of corporate executives on shareholder interests to the exclusion of the wider range of actors that the debate over board design gave voice.

As we have seen, calls for investor stewardship have had modest responses, in part because of the changing conditions in the world of investment. Many of the 'rest of the world' investors are globally active major investment firms with differing motivations for investment and attitudes towards engagement with companies and with the process of codifying corporate governance. Unlike 30 years ago, and more extreme that even 10 years ago, a very large component of the investors active in Britain are 'passive' investors, ones that track an index or some other benchmark, and thus exercise little discretion over what shares they buy or sell. In addition to collective investment vehicles like mutual funds, we also see large volumes of investment in exchange-traded funds using passive investment approaches.

Many of their business models on being low-cost and therefore the cost of engaging with corporations is out of the question. Engagement with the process of codification seems to be slight.

[2] A table detailing the changes in owner-type over the period and an explanatory note is included in Appendix B.

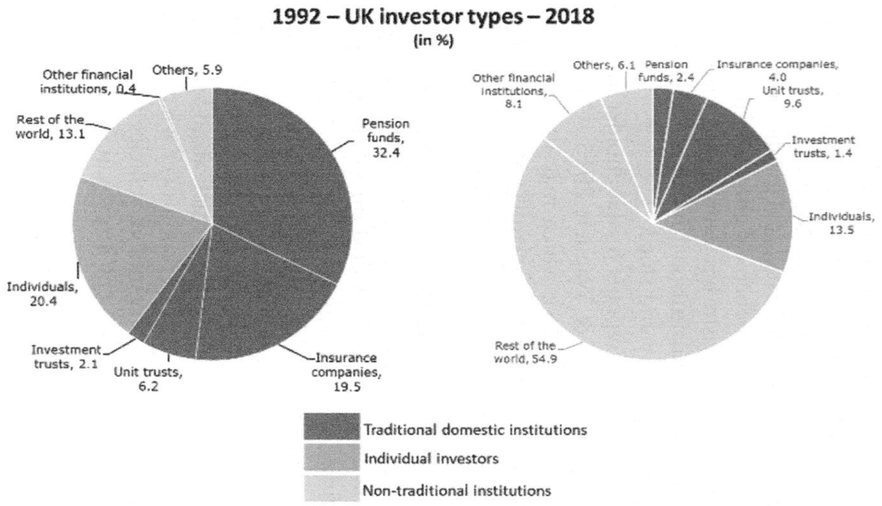

Fig. 8.3 UK equities by ownership type 1992, 2018 (Adapted from ONS data)

And yet a few of them, including one of the very largest firms in the world, BlackRock, have concluded that engagement is necessary. BlackRock has developed a large investor stewardship approach, which is active in Britain and many other countries. It seems to operate on the principle pioneered in the firm we have met above as 'Postel' and 'Hermes' that when you invest widely and hold shares in almost every company, the only way to improve performance of the fund is to improve performance of the market as a whole.[3] Such firms do engage with the process of codification and can have a strong impact when they do.

Another growing component is that of sovereign wealth funds. Many are selective in their investment; they are 'active' investors in contrast to the 'passive' index-trackers. Yet many of those seem to have chosen not to engage with corporations, in part out of concern that their engagement might be viewed as being politically motivated. They may, therefore, also be reluctant to take part in formulating the 'rules of the game' representative in corporate governance codes.

Varied though they are, these investor types seem like to have different motivations for investing than the mainstream UK investors who have been the traditional investor 'voice' in the debates about codification. In the 1990s, UK pension funds invested largely in UK equities to match their assets and liabilities. That alignment can reinforce the idea of psychological ownership, an emotional bond that seems to be a precondition for investor stewardship. For some of the new investor types, by contrast, investment in UK equities is likely to be a more strictly rational decision about asset allocation. Trends in the rest of the investment landscape seem to reinforce that latter approach.

Changing Investment Landscape

Investment decisions are influenced by a variety of other actors, notably the investment banks whose analysts recommend individual shares and trading strategies to large investors. The history of writing the UK corporate governance code shows only modest direct involvement by

[3] The key individuals involved in Hermes Investment Management have long advocated investor stewardship as the only route for passive investors to improve performance (Butler & Wong, 2011; Davis, Lukomnik, & Pitt-Watson, 2006). In 2020 Hermes merged with an American investment firm and listed on the New York Stock Exchange as Federated Hermes Inc.

investment banks. But their indirect influences on the shape in the market context of the code have been great.

When the Cadbury Code was written, investment banking was already undergoing a transformation in their activities from a largely domestic to largely international focus. The de-regulation of the UK market, known as 'Big Bang', in the late 1980s saw US and continental European banks buy much of the old, domestic, family-led merchant banks.

Internationalisation of investment banking helped to spur reform in accounting, and gradually over time financial accounting standards began to converge, culminating after the governance crisis of the early 2000s in the development of International Financial Reporting Standards and their acceptance in the UK and the European Union, as well as much of the world. Somewhat similar changes arose in US and Japanese accounting standards as well. Gone were the quaint and obfuscating standards that had been practised in many countries.

These changes in accounting facilitated comparisons of corporate financial reports across countries and therefore helped investment analysts recommend cross-border trading strategies and conduct international, sector-specific comparisons. That, too, pushed investment in a more international direction, encouraging cross-border share ownership and detaching non-financial reasons for share ownership. It has been matched by changes in how corporations work.

Changing Corporate Landscape

As we have seen, early attention to corporate governance arose in reaction to corporate excesses exposed by the stagflation of the 1970s. That spurred investors—including the early US activists—to press for greater shareholder rights and then to demand changes in how corporations operated. Corporate boards that rebuffed such challenges faced hostile takeover bids in the so-called 'market for corporate control' (Manne, 1965; Walsh & Kosnik, 1993).

A consequence was that companies, first in the US but then in Britain and elsewhere, came to focus their strategies not on diversification but instead of scale economies and management of supply chains. This direction was accompanied by a shift in regulatory philosophy, first in the US and then in Britain, which favoured so-called horizontal mergers—between companies in the same industry and less focus on vertical and unrelated acquisitions.

For analysts, this trend helped to make companies more comparable. For investors, it spurred greater interest in cross-border investment. For corporate boards, it made global operations and pursuit of global customers stronger. But it also made new, globally active companies seek to list their shares and float their bonds in the deepest and most capital markets. The London market was a big beneficiary. These forces combined to create a shift in the nature of the corporations that might be expected to adhere to a UK code of corporate governance.

Respondents to the Cadbury Committee and again in 2003 included representatives of many of the largest UK corporations. By 2010, however, London Stock Exchange listings included many foreign corporations, which sought its liquidity and the legitimacy associated with UK corporate governance. By 2020, the FTSE 100 index bore little resemblance to those of 1992, 2003, or even 2010 in terms of the types of companies, the roots of their businesses, the spread of their customers, and the scale of their operations. Yet these new voices played little role in the 2010 debate or the revisions thereafter.

Implications for Process of Writing the Code

The changes in the corporate governance landscape have implications for the process of writing the code, not least in its legitimacy. Let us be wary about pushing this analysis too far: Many of the participants in the debates we have analysed come from the same general orientations and would seem to share the same interests as the new range of actors. Institutional investors of whatever stripe seek to hold share in corporations that understand their risks. Corporations, whether based in the UK or elsewhere, whether in declining industries or innovative new ones, seek to exploit the opportunities available to greatest effect. Nonetheless, the absence of certain types of voices from the debate over the code, and the domination of traditional voices over the new runs the risk that the legitimacy of the code will diminish.

Legitimacy, as a concept, comes in two varieties: empirically, the broad acceptance of an institution, that is, a set of rules and operating principles; and normatively, a fair reflection of the needs of those involved.

As we have seen in this study, the process of writing the UK code has engaged the voices of a wide range of actors, those central to the field, those on the periphery, and those in between. In the early debates, the code's authors heard a wide variety of those, normatively, with a legitimate claim, and paid the greatest attention to those whose claims were legitimate, urgent, and powerful. The voices whose claims were not recognised in the code could take comfort that the process would give them another chance to revisit their claims. The changes in the landscape suggest, however, that various types of voices—global investors, passive fund managers, foreign companies that list in London, voices that are now legitimate, normatively—take little part in the process.

Moreover, the process of codification won support through its repeated engagement of more peripheral actors. These actors have at times come to identify with the process itself, joining more central actors as part of a corporate governance 'community'. Their voices have been accommodated, yes, but only on the periphery. Institutional arrangements tend to persist, however, and as they do, those actors may come to feel the process itself lacks legitimacy because it is captured by a set of actors in the old centre of the field. The absence of those voices—of those on the periphery and those in the new gravitational centre of the field—from future debates would throw into doubt the empirical legitimacy of the code. The new power structure in investment gives us reasons to think that the old centre may not hold.

References

Battilana, J., & D'Aunno, T. (2009). Institutional work and the paradox of embedded agency. In T. B. Lawrence, R. Suddaby, & B. Leca (Eds.), *Institutional work: Actors and agency in institutional studies of organizations* (pp. 31–58). Cambridge: Cambridge University Press.

Becht, M., Franks, J., Grant, J., & Wagner, H. F. (2015, March). *The returns to hedge fund activism: An international study* (European Corporate Governance Institute (ECGI)—Finance Working Paper No. 402/2014). Retrieved May 21, 2015, from http://dx.doi.org/10.2139/ssrn.2376271.

Bezemer, P.-J., Peij, S. K. L., & Maassen, G. (2014). How two-tier boards can be more effective. *Corporate Governance: The International Journal of Business in Society, 14*(1), 15–31. https://doi.org/10.1108/CG-02-2013-0018.

Butler, P., & Wong, S. C. Y. (2011). Recent trends in institutional investor responsibilities and stewardship. *Pensions: An International Journal, 16*(2), 80–85.

CAMA. (1990). Companies and Allied Matters Act, Chapter 59 of the Laws of the Federation of Nigeria. *Federal Ministry of Justice*. Retrieved May 8, 2020, from http://www.placng.org/lawsofnigeria/laws/C20.pdf.

Cheffins, B. R. (2010). The Stewardship Code's Achilles' Heel. *Modern Law Review, 73*(6), 1004–1025. https://doi.org/10.1111/j.1468-2230.2010.00828.x.

Creed, W. E. D., Dejordy, R., & Lok, J. (2010). Being the change: Resolving institutional contradiction through identity work. *Academy of Management Journal, 53*(6), 1336–1364.

Czarniawska, B., & Joerges, B. (1996). The travel of ideas. In B. Czarniawska & G. Sevon (Eds.), *Translating organizational change* (pp. 13–48). Berlin: de Gruyter.

Davis, S. M., Lukomnik, J., & Pitt-Watson, D. (2006). *The new capitalists: How citizen investors are reshaping the corporate agenda*. Boston: Harvard Business School Press.

Dent, G. W., Jr. (2012). Corporate governance: The Swedish solution. *Florida Law Review, 64*(6), 1633–1668.

DiMaggio, P. J. (1988). Interest and agency in institutional theory. In L. G. Zucker (Ed.), *Institutional patterns and culture* (pp. 3–32). Cambridge, MA: Ballinger.

Ebrahim, A., Battilana, J., & Mair, J. (2014). The governance of social enterprises: Mission drift and accountability challenges in hybrid organizations. *Research in Organizational Behavior, 34,* 81–100. https://doi.org/10.1016/j.riob.2014.09.001.

Fairclough, N. (1992). *Discourse and social change*. Cambridge: Polity Press.

Fama, E. F., & Jensen, M. C. (1983). Agency problems and residual claims. *Journal of Law and Economics, 26*(2), 327–349. https://doi.org/10.1086/467038.

Filatotchev, I., & Dotsenko, O. (2015). Shareholder activism in the UK: types of activists, forms of activism, and their impact on a target's performance. *Journal of Management and Governance, 19*(1), 5–24. https://doi.org/10.1007/s10997-013-9266-5.

Goranova, M., & Ryan, L. V. (2014). Shareholder activism: A multidisciplinary review. *Journal of Management, 40*(5), 1230–1268. https://doi.org/10.1177/0149206313515519.

Greenwood, R., & Hinings, C. R. (1996). Understanding radical organizational change: Bringing together the old and the new institutionalism. *Academy of Management Review, 21*(4), 1022–1054. https://doi.org/10.5465/AMR.1996.9704071862.

Greenwood, R., & Suddaby, R. (2006). Institutional entrepreneurship in mature fields: The Big Five accounting firms. *Academy of Management Journal, 49*(1), 27–48.

Greenwood, R., Suddaby, R., & Hinings, C. R. (2002). Theorizing change: The role of professional associations in the transformation of institutionalized fields. *Academy of Management Journal, 45*(1), 58–80. https://doi.org/10.2307/3069285.

Higgs, D. (2003). *Review of the role and effectiveness of non-executive directors*. Retrieved October 15, 2006, from http://www.ecgi.org/codes/documents/higgsreport.pdf.

Hinings, C. R., Brown, J. L., & Greenwood, R. (1991). Change in an autonomous professional organization. *Journal of Management Studies, 28*(4), 375–393. https://doi.org/10.1111/j.1467-6486.1991.tb00287.x.

Hood, C. (1995). The 'new public management' in the 1980s: Variations on a theme. *Accounting, Organizations and Society, 20*(2), 93–109. https://doi.org/10.1016/0361-3682(93)E0001-W.

Jensen, M. C., & Meckling, W. H. (1976). Theory of the firm: Managerial behavior, agency costs and ownership structure. *The Journal of Financial Economics, 3*(4), 305–360. https://doi.org/10.1016/0304-405X(76)90026-X.

Lawrence, T. B., & Suddaby, R. (2006). Institutions and institutional work. In S. Clegg, C. Hardy, T. B. Lawrence, & W. R. Nord (Eds.), *The Sage handbook of organization studies* (2nd ed., pp. 215–254). London: Sage.

Lok, J. (2010). Institutional logics as identity projects. *Academy of Management Journal, 53*(6), 1305–1335. https://doi.org/10.5465/AMJ.2010.57317866.

Maassen, G. F., & van den Bosch, F. A. J. (1999). On the supposed independence of two-tier boards: formal structure and reality in the Netherlands. *Corporate Governance: an International Review, 7*(1), 31–37. https://doi.org/10.1111/1467-8683.00126.

Manne, H. G. (1965). Mergers and the market for corporate control. *Journal of Political Economy, 73*(2), 110–120. https://doi.org/10.2307/1829527.

McNulty, T., & Nordberg, D. (2016). Ownership, activism and engagement: Institutional investors as active owners. *Corporate Governance: An International Review, 24*(3), 346–358. https://doi.org/10.1111/corg.12143.

Meyer, J. W., & Rowan, B. (1977). Institutionalized organizations: Formal structure as myth and ceremony. *American Journal of Sociology, 83*(2), 340–363.

Mitchell, R. K., Agle, B. R., & Wood, Donna J. (1997). Toward a theory of stakeholder identification and salience: Defining the principle of who and what really counts. *Academy of Management Review, 22*(4), 853–886. https://doi.org/10.5465/AMR.1997.9711022105.

Nachemson-Ekwall, S., & Mayer, C. (2018, May). Nomination committees and corporate governance: Lessons from Sweden and the UK. *Saïd Business School WP 2018–12*. Retrieved September 6, 2018, from https://ssrn.com/abstract=3170397.

Nordberg, D. (2017). Board ethos and institutional work: Developing a corporate governance identity through developing the UK code. *Economics and Business Review, 3[17]*(1), 73–96. https://doi.org/10.18559/ebr.2017.1.4.

Nordberg, D. (2018). Edging toward 'reasonably' good corporate governance. *Philosophy of Management, 17*(3), 353–371. https://doi.org/10.1007/s40926-017-0083-9.

Nordberg, D. (2020). Book review: Daniel S. Milo, good enough—The tolerance of mediocrity in nature and society. *Organization Studies, 41*(6), 899–901. https://doi.org/10.1177/0170840619871177.

Nordberg, D., & McNulty, T. (2013). Creating better boards through codification: Possibilities and limitations in UK corporate governance, 1992–2010. *Business History, 55*(3), 348–374. https://doi.org/10.1080/00076791.2012.712964.

North, D. C. (1990). *Institutions, institutional change and economic performance*. Cambridge: Cambridge University Press.

O'Neill, O. (2002). *A question of trust: The BBC Reith Lectures 2002*. Cambridge: Cambridge University Press.

ONS. (2020, January). *Ownership of UK quoted shares, 2018*. Statistical Bulletin of the UK Office of National Statistics. Retrieved April 3, 2020, from https://www.ons.gov.uk/economy/investmentspensionsandtrusts/bulletins/ownershipofukquotedshares/2018/pdf.

Rao, H., & Giorgi, S. (2006). Code breaking: How entrepreneurs exploit cultural logics to generate institutional change. *Research in Organizational Behavior, 27*, 269–304. https://doi.org/10.1016/S0191-3085(06)27007-2.

Roach, L. (2011). The UK stewardship code. *Journal of Corporate Law Studies, 11*(2), 463–493.

Soin, K., & Huber, C. (2013). The sedimentation of an institution: Changing governance in U.K. financial services. *Journal of Management Inquiry, 22*(3), 260–280. https://doi.org/10.1177/1056492612467510.

Suddaby, R., & Greenwood, R. (2005). Rhetorical strategies of legitimacy. *Administrative Science Quarterly, 50*(1), 35–67.

Veldman, J., & Willmott, H. C. (2016). The cultural grammar of governance: The UK code of corporate governance, reflexivity, and the limits of 'soft' regulation. *Human Relations, 69*(3), 581–603. https://doi.org/10.1177/0018726715593160.

Walsh, J. P., & Kosnik, R. D. (1993). Corporate raiders and their disciplinary role in the market for corporate control. *Academy of Management Journal, 36*(4), 671–700. https://doi.org/10.2307/256755.

Westphal, J. D., & Graebner, M. (2010). A matter of appearances: How corporate leaders manage the impressions of financial analysts about the conduct of their boards. *Academy of Management Journal, 53*(1), 15–44.

Wong, S. C. Y. (2010). *Why stewardship is proving elusive for institutional investors* (Northwestern Law & Econ Research Paper No. 10–28). Retrieved August 28, 2012, from http://ssrn.com/abstract=1635662.

CHAPTER 9

Conclusions

Abstract The Cadbury Code was born in an emergency, and through various revisions and iterations has become part of the fabric not just of corporate life in the UK, but also around the world and in other domains. This recalls the benefits—in strengthening board process—but also reflects on its shortcomings. It asks practitioners and scholars to consider how the shifting context might affect how suitable its remedies are for the problems of corporate governance.

Keywords Implications for practice · Implications for scholarship · Implications beyond the UK corporate world

Starting with the Cadbury Report, the UK code of corporate governance has evolved gradually over the past three decades. Incremental changes have incorporated ideas about wider aspects of the actions, activities, and ethos of boards. New points of emphasis have emerged in the language used to discuss corporate governance itself. Through a deliberate policy of regular consultations and revisions, incremental changes in its provisions have reflected the changing understanding of what makes a board work well, changes that then inform the new consensus. While the code thus reflects the emerged consensus, its institutionalisation inhibits changes in what that consensus considers legitimate. In embracing explanation as a form of compliance, it left the door open for experimentation. In its

D. Nordberg, *The Cadbury Code and Recurrent Crisis*,
https://doi.org/10.1007/978-3-030-55222-0_9

increasing articulation of good governance, however, it draws attention away from the unfamiliar and thus from the possibility of experimenting. If compliance with the institution suffices, the thoughtfulness of ethical decision-making is not required.

Codifying corporate governance has brought many benefits to UK listed companies and to the many other countries and sectors where its principles have been followed. But it also created problems. Strategists generally agree that competitive advantage arises from the distinctiveness of the company, whether in its products and services (Porter, 1980) or in the resource base on which its future is built (Barney, 1991). Used in a mechanistic way, the code of corporate governance seems to ask the top decision-making body of companies to be the same.

As this study has shown, the UK code has attempted, despite its layers of prescription, to use explanation as a form of compliance and thus to keep the door open for distinctiveness. Whether it has succeeded in that attempt is less than clear. Challenge is stronger, but the work of boards seems also to have become more routine.

This study has examined how the debate over the UK code of corporate governance created a discourse of corporate governance and set the language in which governance would be conducted, and then shows how it developed over time. In doing so it shows how the process of writing the code can consolidate power, gain legitimacy, and inform conduct. These point to the study's three main contributions.

First, the history of the code shows how, repeatedly, the political context created a power vacuum that permitted codification to take the place of legislation and regulation. That contest favoured central actors—institutional investors even more than corporations—over others. But through their participation in the process peripheral actors found their voices hear, repeatedly, and thus in part legitimated. Engagement with the process led to identity formation for the individuals involved and built up a vocabulary of corporate governance that informed the discourse in which subsequent debate would take place. That discourse helped to solidify the code, but the process of regular revision helped to keep ideas rejected alive. Codification of corporate governance remained, therefore, a thoughtful process even if the practice in some companies became unthinking compliance. The experimentation that Sir Adrian Cadbury contemplated and that the 'comply-or-explain' provision enabled was only modest. Here codification failed to achieve the aims of the process by institutionalising certain practices in corporations. It also concentrated power in the hands of certain actors, even as the market context in which they operated undermined the basis of the legitimacy of their power.

Second, it shows theoretically that the institutional work of actors engaging can configure power. But in the process, while some logics may be blended in the process, others are suspended—not put into action but not vanquished. Legitimated through debate, they can resurface and perhaps gain ground later. This suspension of a logic, coupled with a mechanism to prompt revisiting the arrangements, meant that a defeated logic remained alive and retained legitimacy. That logics were suspended but not defeated has left the door open to continuing institutional entrepreneurship, facilitating gradual change and sustaining the code's legitimacy. This idea of institutional logics in suspension may have applicability in circumstances well beyond the scope of corporate governance or UK institutional arrangements.

Third, these insights have practical significance by showing how consultations create discourses that effect change, and how by creating in effect perpetual consultations and repeated revisions to the rules, the process itself becomes institutionalised. While specific rules may change in response to major exogenous shocks, the process remains legitimate and persists.

The UK experience of codifying corporate governance has influenced practice in many other jurisdictions. Shortly after the Cadbury Code was issued, industry organisations in France banded together to create the Vienot Code (CNPF, 1995). Germany created a code of corporate governance that echoed many of the UK provisions despite its legal requirements for a dual board structure and *Mitbestimmung* rights mandating employee representation on boards (Cromme Commission, 2002/2007). South Africa seemed to go into competition with the UK over which would develop in code provisions (SAIoD, 1994, 2016), winning plaudits from backers of strong codification of social responsibility. The European Corporate Governance Institute lists hundreds of national codes, many of which follow the broad outline established in the UK.[1]

But the processes developed by the Cadbury Committee and then modified and standardised over time have analogues in other settings

[1] See https://ecgi.global/content/codes for details.

as well. In Cadbury's two phases, in the Higgs Review and the subsequent FRC consultation, and in the three rounds of the post-financial crisis review, we can see echoes of other consultations approaches. One example was the 'Lamfalussy process' used in formulating financial regulation in the European Union in the late 1990s and early 2000s. It followed a similar formal, multi-level, and iterated approach (Gari & Lastra, 2009; Schaub, 2005). Like the case of UK corporate governance, its successive phases moved from broad to narrow and won legitimacy for often controversial steps by repeatedly engaging central and peripheral actors in the process.

The present study suggests that by engaging in the process of code-writing, actors create a new logic, arising more from a collective stance rather than the narrower interests and a new community. They forge a new identity—a community of corporate governance—oriented and making the system of governance work well. But the consultations have done more than that.

The development of the code, especially during the revisions not analysed here, has added successive layers of mechanisms of good governance. They address potentially important areas of director diversity, public reporting of board activities, the definition of independence, and articulation of what good explanations of non-compliance should be.

These layers have added to the stipulations of the Cadbury Code, feeding into systems for tracking and scoring compliance, and into mathematical models to governance portfolio management that channel investment flows. Such devices may well prove successful—at the portfolio level—in increasing the performance of a portfolio of shares. But the metrics they generate are very far removed from the choices an individual board of directors needs to make, about individual business decisions, or about the individuals to be selected to fill the one vacancy on a corporate board. The code of corporate governance must, therefore, have different significance to corporations and institutional investors.

The opening sections of the 2010 code, which urged greater flexibility, wider use of explanations, and greater understanding from investors, encouraged boards to attend those layers but not become fixated on them. They urged directors and investors alike to focus on the relational elements that its author, Sir Christopher Hogg, felt was its core. But newspaper accounts at the time nonetheless focused on the provisions it added (Sanderson & Burgess, 2010; Wilson, 2010). What has received less scrutiny is whether these layers may duplicate or even impede each other in their effects on how boards work. If no one size fits all (Anderson & Gupta, 2013; Pye & Camm, 2003), the practical question for boards and investors may be 'what fits well enough?'

There is little reason—in this study or in the general discourse about corporate governance—to doubt that the UK code has been a success in raising awareness of the issues of governance in all types of organisations. In the UK, the broad principles outlined in the corporate governance code have informed new configurations in the public sector. Boards of devolved units of the National Health Service follow a code with strong parallels to corporations. Under the Labour government in the early 2000s, leadership structures of central government departments created new posts for 'non-executive directors'. Even the British House of Commons—an odd non-organisation—issued a corporate governance statement and undertook evaluations of the effectiveness of their operating boards (Nordberg, 2013, 2014). UK charities, too, have a code of corporate governance based on similar principles (Charity Governance Code Steering Group, 2017).

It has also increased the attention of corporate directors to the details of the companies on whose boards they serve. Directors work harder now, pay greater attention to detail, and demand a higher quality and volume of information from the management teams under their direction. Directors are also better trained in the skills of corporate direction and about the mechanisms available to assert control. As the implementation of codes like the UK Corporate Governance Code has spread to other jurisdictions and other forms of organisations, those boards are almost certainly working harder and smarter.

Yet the trigger for the Cadbury Code and both its major revisions, the codes examined in this study, lay in corporate collapse. It may be too much to ask a code to eradicate greed or the guilt that lies behind the decision to cover up a mistake. Nor is it obvious that law or regulation, while providing a stronger institutional framework, would retain enough flexibility to accommodate the complexities associated with a wide range of businesses, operating in different market contexts and with differing resources bases. A code that emphasises 'explanation' as a form of 'compliance' may not either. In some ways, the UK code became a box-ticking exercise. If 'comply or explain' comes to be regarded in practice 'comply or else', then it has delivered a one-size-fits-all solution that fits no one particularly well (Arcot, Bruno, & Faure-Grimaud, 2010; cf. Dowell, Shackell, & Stuart, 2011; Hertig, 2005), let alone every business type

Prime Minister May felt compelled to resign, and with it went her ambitions for German-style co-determination of corporate boards. Will a new logic appear, embracing the changed context and the new actors?

Since the Carillion disaster, further corporate failures have occurred, privatised rail franchises have collapsed, private providers of social care services have been driven out of business through malpractice and excessive debt, leaving people for whom they were supposed to care, in exchange for public funding, in a lurch. These cases have been somewhat less spectacular than Carillion but damaging, nonetheless.

The UK Corporate Governance Code has become, in practice, something more like the 'rigid set of rules' the 2010 code had warned against. The 'roads not taken' include the options of other models of board design, and not just German-style two-tier ones. They include choices of board composition and processes that might have fostered at once both greater collegiality *and* greater boardroom challenge. In short, might practitioners and regulators alike might start to pursue much more eagerly the experimentation that Sir Adrian Cadbury mooted in his handwritten notations? Might experimentation grow by embracing 'explanation' as a form of compliance?

A Glimpse of the Future

For a decade or more, the number of companies listed on the London Stock Exchange has been falling, depleted through foreign takeovers, private equity raids, and a lack of new listings, particularly of domestic firms. Companies declining to list often cite corporate governance compliance as one of the impediments to raising funds on public markets. Are these the signs of a healthy system of corporate governance?

In the early months of 2020, the arrival of the coronavirus pandemic rocked Britain and the rest of the world. This was not a crisis in corporate governance *per se*, but it put many corporations into crisis. As revenues collapsed and customers stayed indoors, airlines grounded their fleets, buses, and rail franchises cancelled services, retailers and restaurant chains fell into administration, and the state took control of large swathes of the UK economy. At the time of writing the final parts of this study, it was impossible to do more than speculate about the consequences of this pandemic for the ethics of corporate governance and the ethos of boardrooms, the politics and power in capital markets, or even how formal institutions like the Financial Reporting council or company law will develop, let alone the less formal ones like the corporate governance code. Is this the 'precipitating jolt' that might force a rethink of an institution like the corporate governance code? Time will tell.

References

Booth, R., & Nordberg, D. (2018, February). *Response to UK corporate governance consultation paper 2018*. Submission to the UK Financial Reporting Council. Retrieved February 28, 2018, from https://www.frc.org.uk/getattachment/0b954635-be94-470b-af5e-984c26710352/Carey-Group;.aspx.

Business Roundtable. (2019, August). *Statement on the purpose of a corporation*. Retrieved August 26, 2019, from https://opportunity.businessroundtable.org/wp-content/uploads/2019/08/Business-Roundtable-Statement-on-the-Purpose-of-a-Corporation-with-Signatures.pdf.

Financial Times. (2019, October 13). *How to build a more responsible corporate capitalism*. Statement of the FT Editorial Board. Retrieved April 6, 2020, from https://www.ft.com/content/8b282346-eaa3-11e9-85f4-d00e5018f061.

MacAvoy, P., & Millstein, I. (2003). *The recurrent crisis in corporate governance*. Basingstoke: Palgrave Macmillan.

O'Connor, S., & Brunsden, J. (2016, July). Businesses wary of Theresa May's board reforms. *FT.com*. Retrieved July 11, 2016, from https://www.ft.com/content/09fc5360-4780-11e6-b387-64ab0a67014c.

Strine, L. E., Jr. (2019, October). *Toward fair and sustainable capitalism: A comprehensive proposal to help American workers, restore fair gainsharing between employees and shareholders, and increase American competitiveness by reorienting our corporate governance system toward sustainable long-term growth and encouraging investments in America's future* (Harvard Law School Discussion Paper No. 1018; SSRN eLibrary). Retrieved October 3, 2019, from https://ssrn.com/abstract=3461924.

UK Government. (2019a, March 11). *Audit regime in the UK to be transformed with new regulator*. Retrieved April 6, 2020, from https://www.gov.uk/government/news/audit-regime-in-the-uk-to-be-transformed-with-new-regulator.

UK Government. (2019b, April 18). *CMA recommends shake-up of UK audit market*. News release of the UK Competition and Markets Authority. Retrieved April 6, 2020, from https://www.gov.uk/government/news/cma-recommends-shake-up-of-uk-audit-market.

Appendix A—Research Methods

Following the approach of Fairclough (1992), this study examines how a discourse of corporate governance develops from the rhetoric of debate, shaping the social context. It focuses on the debates over three versions of the UK code that occurred in response to major crises in corporate governance, when the threat to institutionalised practices was most acute: the Cadbury Code (1992), the post-Enron Combined Code (FRC, 2003), and the renamed UK Corporate Governance Code (FRC, 2010), based on documents generated by the consultation processes, which varied over time: from the informal first round of the Cadbury discussions to more formal second round; 'fatal flaws only' review in 2003; and a three-phase formal consultation conducted by Sir Christopher Hogg, who chaired the FRC in the 2009–2010 period and had advised the Cadbury Committee in 1992.

There are drawbacks to such a document-driven analysis, of course. First, in the 'small worlds' (Kogut, 2012) of corporate governance and company boards, it is reasonable to assume that many discussions took place that did not find their way into formal records. Second, in some cases, formal texts may have been sanitised before submission, under the watchful eye of corporate counsel. Third, many private and semi-public meetings will have taken place, the content of which could have influenced the writing of the code without finding their way into formal submissions.

D. Nordberg, *The Cadbury Code and Recurrent Crisis*,
https://doi.org/10.1007/978-3-030-55222-0

This study was motivated in part by the author's own participation in several such events in both 2003 and 2009–2010, and by a lengthy discussion with Sir Christopher Hogg after he had conducted the third of these major exercises. While the analysis presented here focuses on the documents, these experiences provide scope for some triangulation from the documents. In the case of the Cadbury Report, Sir Adrian's own notations on the documents capture some of the less formal aspects of the process in 1991–1992.

Specifically, the consultations analysed for this study were (1) formal submissions following the Cadbury draft in May 1992, as well as related material from before the draft; (2) the 'fatal flaws only' consultation after the Higgs Review in 2003; and (3) all three phases of the 2009–2010 consultation. Almost three hundred Cadbury documents were examined closely, selected after reading through the two-and-a-half thousand paper records held at the Cadbury archive at the University of Cambridge (referenced with numbers beginning with CAD). Of those 201 were also downloaded from the online archive.

Records of the 2003 review are less comprehensive. The FRC provided some documents in hard copy from the 'fatal flaws only' consultation after the Higgs Review in 2003; others were uncovered through internet searches of legacy pages on the FRC website. In all some 123 documents were located, and after filtering for salience, 73 documents were used in the initial analysis. These give a wide, if perhaps incomplete picture.[1] This was intended to be a quick review, and nonetheless the FRC received well over 100 submissions. It seems reasonable to conclude they offer a rounded view of the opinions expressed. The author also participated in debates held during the consultation about how to bring the Higgs recommendations into the code.

Documents from the 2009–2010 consultations were harvested contemporaneously from the FRC website. The first, open consultation involved 105 public submissions; another 89 from the second phase, after publication of the Walker Review (2009); and 119 from the consultation on the FRC new draft code.

The examination of the texts proceeded using critical discourse analysis. It involved an initial reading of all available texts, which ranged from

[1] The study did not look at the Higgs Review itself, only at the consultation that followed. Reflections on Higgs can be seen in the article by Roberts, McNulty, and Stiles (2005), who worked on the review.

one to 35 pages, followed by iterative reading of a sample selected on two theoretical grounds. First, the study applied a criterion of salience (Mitchell, Agle, & Wood, 1997). Assuming all respondent voices were legitimate, the analysis took the centrality of actors as an indicator of power and force of the language to indicate urgency. This led to identification of texts using stronger rhetoric, the ones more likely, that is, to impress the codes' authors.

Second, texts were selected from actors in different parts of the investment chain running from individual savers through banks and brokerages to investment management. It also examined contributions from peripheral actors, who might offer different or dissonant voices. Powerful, central actors can be agents of institutional change (Greenwood & Suddaby, 2006), while peripheral players effect change through importing ideas from adjacent fields (Rao & Giorgi, 2006). This led to close analysis of the rhetoric in texts that showed salience and diversity of position in investment. That was followed by an iterative reading of other texts to ensure the selection reflected the weight of the evidence.

Using Nvivo software, initial coding tracked texts for terms commonplace in corporate governance, including in the literature on agency theory, stewardship, stakeholder and resource dependency, and for first-level concepts like boards and investors. Also recorded were less-tangible concepts, including board structure, independence and behaviour that figure prominently in the code texts themselves as well as in the literature. Axial coding followed, showing links between concepts (e.g. structure enhances accountability, or structure constrains strategic choice). In the identification of themes, special attention was paid to emotive language, metaphor, and other rhetorical devices that could influence the readers who were also acting as authors of the code. By sheer volume, the Cadbury documentation offers the richest source of the areas of conflict. Its novelty stirred anxiety. For subsequent revisions, the code had become accepted if perhaps not entirely taken for granted.

References

Cadbury, A. (1992). *The financial aspects of corporate governance*. Retrieved September 1, 2015, from http://www.ecgi.org/codes/documents/cadbury.pdf.

Fairclough, N. (1992). *Discourse and social change*. Cambridge: Polity Press.

FRC. (2003). *Combined code on corporate governance*. UK Financial Reporting Council. Retrieved June 20, 2006, from http://www.frc.org.uk/documents/pagemanager/frc/Web%20Optimised%20Combined%20Code%203rd%20proof.pdf.

FRC. (2010). *The UK corporate governance code*. UK Financial Reporting Council. Retrieved May 29, 2010, from http://www.frc.org.uk/documents/pagemanager/Corporate_Governance/UK%20Corp%20Gov%20Code%20June%202010.pdf.

Greenwood, R., & Suddaby, R. (2006). Institutional entrepreneurship in mature fields: The Big Five accounting firms. *Academy of Management Journal, 49*(1), 27–48.

Kogut, B. (Ed.). (2012). *The small worlds of corporate governance*. Cambridge: MIT Press.

Mitchell, R. K., Agle, B. R., & Wood, D. J. (1997). Toward a theory of stakeholder identification and salience: Defining the principle of who and what really counts. *Academy of Management Review, 22*(4), 853–886. https://doi.org/10.5465/amr.1997.9711022105.

Rao, H., & Giorgi, S. (2006). Code breaking: How entrepreneurs exploit cultural logics to generate institutional change. *Research in Organizational Behavior, 27*, 269–304. https://doi.org/10.1016/s0191-3085(06)27007-2.

Roberts, J., McNulty, T., & Stiles, P. (2005). Beyond agency conceptions of the work of the non-executive director: Creating accountability in the boardroom. *British Journal of Management, 16*(S1), S5–S26.

Walker, D. (2009, November 26). A review of corporate governance in UK banks and other financial industry entities: Final recommendations. *HM Treasury Independent Reviews*. Retrieved November 26, 2009, from http://www.hm-treasury.gov.uk/d/walker_review_consultation_160709.pdf.

Appendix B—UK Share Ownership

Table B.1 gives the historical record of ownership during the period under review in this book. Mainstream domestic institutional investors became

Table B.1 The UK share ownership by type of investor, in %

	Cadbury Code 1992	*Combined Code 1998*	*Higgs Review 2003*	*Financial crisis 2008*	*New CG code 2010*	*Latest data 2018*
Pension funds	32.4	21.7	16.0	12.8	5.6	2.4
Insurance companies	19.5	21.6	17.3	13.4	8.8	4.0
Unit trusts	6.2	2.0	1.5	1.8	8.8	9.6
Investment trusts	2.1	1.3	1.7	1.9	2.1	1.4
Individuals	20.4	16.7	14.9	10.2	10.2	13.5
Rest of the world	13.1	30.7	36.1	41.5	43.4	54.9
Other financial institutions	0.4	2.7	8.3	10.0	12.3	8.1
Others	5.9	3.5	4.2	8.4	8.7	6.1
Total	100	100	100	100	100	100

Source Office of National Statistics data

D. Nordberg, *The Cadbury Code and Recurrent Crisis*,
https://doi.org/10.1007/978-3-030-55222-0

the dominant holders of UK equities during the 1970s and 1980s, as private pension provision took the lion's share of investment in old-age provision beyond the basic state pension. Part of that growth appeared in the category of 'insurance companies', which began to market defined contribution pension instruments to individuals who were not covered by large corporate defined benefit plans.

The category 'other financial institutions' includes UK-based alternative investments, including hedge funds. 'Rest of the world' is all foreign investors, though the vast majority of this represents institutional investment by both foreign mainstream investors, including European and US-based mutual funds; sovereign wealth funds from Norway, the Gulf states and elsewhere; and non-UK hedge funds.

The decline in market share of pension funds is particularly steep. That seems to reflect in part the decline in availability of corporate defined benefit plans to new employees and their replacement with defined contribution plans. As the membership of such pension plans moved closer to retirement and death, pension funds generally invest more conservatively, increasing their holding of fixed income investments (bonds), while reducing their investment in equities. A related contributory factor was the decline in trade unions in the UK over the period.

Over this time pension funds also reduced direct investment, choosing increasingly to outsource asset management to investment professionals from the other investor types. They included 'rest of the world' investors and hedge funds, but also domestic fund management organisations, including insurance companies. A lively debate ensued concerning the legal and moral differences between 'asset managers' and 'asset owners' (Butler & Wong, 2011; Investment Association, 2015; ISG, 2017; Johnson, Williams, & Aguilera, 2019). Such outsourced investment meant that the name of the entity on the share register was different from that of the beneficiary.

Such outsourcing also created a longer chain of investment separating the end-beneficiary—the saver or the pensioner—from the object of the investment—the corporation (Kay, 2012). This development became increasingly a concern during the financial crisis and led to the development of a UK Stewardship Code (FRC, 2010, 2012), an attempt to mirror the 'successes' for the corporate governance code to address the weaknesses in accountability along the investment chain (Cheffins, 2010; McNulty & Nordberg, 2016; Reisberg, 2015; Wong, 2015).

References

Butler, P., & Wong, S. C. Y. (2011). Recent trends in institutional investor responsibilities and stewardship. *Pensions: An International Journal, 16*(2), 80–85.

Cheffins, B. R. (2010). The Stewardship Code's Achilles' Heel. *Modern Law Review, 73*(6), 1004–1025. https://doi.org/10.1111/j.1468-2230.20, https://doi.org/10.00828.x.

FRC. (2010). The UK Stewardship Code. *UK Financial Reporting Council.* Retrieved July 2, 2010, from http://www.frc.org.uk/images/uploaded/documents/UK%20Stewardship%20Code%20July%2020103.pdf.

FRC. (2012, September). The UK Stewardship Code. *UK Financial Reporting Council.* Retrieved September 28, 2012, from http://www.frc.org.uk/getattachment/e2db042e-120b-4e4e-bdc7-d540923533a6/UK-Stewardship-Code-September-2012.aspx.

Investment Association. (2015, June). Adherence to the FRC's Stewardship Code at September 2014. Retrieved August 11, 2015, from http://www.theinvestmentassociation.org/assets/files/surveys/20150526-fullstewardshipcode.pdf.

ISG. (2017, January). Stewardship framework for institutional investors. *Investor Stewardship Group policy statement.* Retrieved February 5, 2017, from https://www.isgframework.org/stewardship-principles/.

Johnson, K., Williams, C., & Aguilera, R. (2019). Proxy voting reform: What is on the agenda, what is not on the agenda, and why it matters for asset owners. *Boston University Law Review, 99*(3), 1347–1366.

Kay, J. (2012, July). *The Kay review of UK equity markets and long-term decision making—Final report*. Consultation of the UK Department of Business, Innovation and Skills. Retrieved July 23, 2012, from http://www.bis.gov.uk/assets/biscore/business-law/docs/k/12-917-kay-review-of-equity-markets-final-report.pdf.

McNulty, T., & Nordberg, D. (2016). Ownership, activism and engagement: Institutional investors as active owners. *Corporate Governance: An International Review, 24*(3), 346–358. https://doi.org/10.1111/corg.12143.

Reisberg, A. (2015). The UK Stewardship Code: On the road to nowhere? *Journal of Corporate Law Studies, 15*(2), 217–253. https://doi.org/10.1080/14735970.2015.1044771.

Wong, S. C.Y. (2015, September). *Is institutional investor Stewardship still elusive?* Northwestern Law & Econ Research Paper No. 15–16. Retrieved August 2, 2016, from http://ssrn.com/abstract=2654229.

Index

D. Nordberg, *The Cadbury Code and Recurrent Crisis*,
https://doi.org/10.1007/978-3-030-55222-0

The manufacturer's authorised representative in the EU is Springer Nature Customer Service Centre GmbH, Europaplatz 3, 69115 Heidelberg, Germany. If you have any concerns regarding our products, please contact ProductSafety@springernature.com

Printed and bound by CPI Group (UK) Ltd, Croydon, CR0 4YY
30/09/2026
02225666-0014